Supporting the Family Business

This fully updated second edition provides evidence-based, solution-focused techniques for applying coaching in family business settings.

Manfusa Shams has demonstrated the critical connection between coaching skills, family business functions, experiential and reflective learning. Edition updates incorporate material on homeworking, family dynamics, team coaching, online business coaching. Featuring accessible case studies, practical tools and techniques, all chapters showcase how practitioners can learn from the coaching practice and the skills, competencies and experiences needed to provide effective family business coaching. The book particularly emphasises interventions which are compatible with virtual coaching to support family businesses to achieve business goals and to retain their competitive edge.

Supporting the Family Business is a valuable guide for the continued professional development of practitioners working with family businesses, as well as members of family businesses seeking new learning and development opportunities.

Manfusa Shams, PhD, is a consulting editor for "The Coaching Psychologist", book series editor for "Coaching Psychology for Professional Practice" and an editorial board member for "International Coaching Psychology Review". She teaches at the Open University, England, UK.

The Professional Coaching Series

This series brings together leading exponents and researchers in the coaching field to provide a definitive set of core texts important to the development of the profession. It aims to meet two needs - a professional series that provides the core texts that are theoretically and experimentally grounded, and a practice series covering forms of coaching based in evidence. Together they provide a complementary framework to introduce, promote and enhance the development of the coaching profession.

Titles in the series:

Swings and Roundabouts: A Self-Coaching Workbook for Parents and Those Considering Becoming Parents
By Agnes Bamford

Internal Coaching: The Inside Story
By Katharine St John-Brooks

Coaching in Education: Getting Better Results for Students, Educators, and Parents
By Christian van Nieuwerburgh

Coaching in the Family Owned Business: A Path to Growth
By Manfusa Shams and David A. Lane

Integrated Experiential Coaching: Becoming an Executive Coach
By Lloyd Chapman

The Art of Inspired Living: Coach Yourself with Positive Psychology
By Sarah Corrie

For further information about this series please visit
www.routledge.com/The-Professional-Coaching-Series/book-series/KARNPROFC

Supporting the Family Business

A Coaching Practitioner's Handbook

Second Edition

Manfusa Shams

Routledge
Taylor & Francis Group

LONDON AND NEW YORK

Cover image: © Getty Images

Second edition published 2022
by Routledge
2 Park Square, Milton Park, Abingdon, Oxon, OX14 4RN

and by Routledge
605 Third Avenue, New York, NY 10158

Routledge is an imprint of the Taylor & Francis Group, an informa business

First edition published by Routledge 2015

British Library Cataloguing-in-Publication Data
A catalogue record for this book is available from the British Library

Library of Congress Cataloging-in-Publication Data
Names: Shams, Manfusa, author.
Title: Supporting the family business : a coaching
practitioner's handbook / Manfusa Shams.
Description: Second edition. | Abingdon, Oxon; New York, NY: Routledge, 2022. |
Series: The professional coaching series |
Includes bibliographical references and index. |
Identifiers: LCCN 2021035593 (print) | LCCN 2021035594 (ebook) |
ISBN 9781032005720 (hardback) | ISBN 9781032005713 (paperback) |
ISBN 9781003174721 (ebook)
Subjects: LCSH: Family-owned business enterprises–Psychological aspects. |
Executive coaching.
Classification: LCC HD62.25.S5185 2022 (print) |
LCC HD62.25 (ebook) | DDC 658/.04–dc23
LC record available at https://lccn.loc.gov/2021035593
LC ebook record available at https://lccn.loc.gov/2021035594

ISBN: 978-1-03-200572-0 (hbk)
ISBN: 978-1-03-200571-3 (pbk)
ISBN: 978-1-00-317472-1 (ebk)

DOI: 10.4324/9781003174721

Typeset in Times New Roman
by Newgen Publishing UK

For my parents, especially my mother, one of the few women who completed higher education in science during British rule of India, and my father, a renowned Judge—for their unlimited love, encouragement, inspiration & support.

—Manfusa, June 2021. England.

Contents

About the contributors

Manfusa Shams, is a fellow of the Higher Education Academy, UK, and obtained her PhD in Occupational Psychology from the Institute of Work Psychology, Sheffield University, England. Among her numerous major publications are, *Coaching in the Family Owned Business: A Path to Growth* (Routledge), Supporting the family business: a coaching practitioner's handbook (Routledge), and *Developments in Work and Organizational Psychology: Implications for International Business* (Elsevier/Emerald), and two edited leading journals, *The Psychologist* (special issue) and *Asian Journal of Social Psychology* (special issue). Manfusa is a mentor and an experienced author, editor, supervisor, peer-reviewer and group facilitator. She is an associate fellow, chartered psychologist and a chartered scientist of the British Psychological Society. She is a series editor for *Coaching Psychology for Professional Practice*, a consulting editor for *The Coaching Psychologist*, and an editorial board member of the *International Coaching Psychology Review* journal. She served as a Host for East of England practitioners peer practice group. She holds academic positions in the Open University and Reading University, England. She is also working for a number of leading international and professional organisations.

Janey Howl is an independent psychologist, coach, facilitator, mentor and writer. As an associate fellow of the British Psychological Society, a longstanding associate of Hult Ashridge Executive Education and a founder member of the Association for Business Psychology, Janey has a considerable track record in helping corporate leaders and their teams to achieve extraordinary results. Bringing eclectic ideas, inspirations, thoughts and narratives to her professional practice, Janey has supported numerous people, of all ages and from all walks of life, in finding, creating, and some-times exiting, the job of their dreams. Currently completing a doctorate in Health Psychology, Janey's focus is on workplace toxicity, redressing the human costs of endemic stress, systemic bullying and harassment, plus mitigating the impact of sustained virtual working occasioned by a global pandemic. By providing tools and practices that combine cutting-edge science with the wisdom of the ages, her Reboot Programme is a unique evidence-based integrated mind–body approach that empowers individuals and organisations to become healthier, more productive, more creative and ultimately sustainable.

Julia Lampshire is an independent psychologist having previously worked as a director in a psychology consultancy and as a partner in an international HR consultancy where she led the UK organisational development team. She works as a business psychologist, coach and psychotherapist. She is chartered by the British Psychological Society and is an associate fellow. She is also a member of the Special Group for Coaching Psychologists and the International Society for Coaching Psychology and, as a therapist, is registered through the UK Council for Psychotherapy. She is the co-author of the CIPD *Coaching Toolkit* and has written two coaching DVDs, *Coaching Skills for Line Managers* and *Communicating in Difficult Situations*.

Declan Woods is an accredited aster Coach, a chartered and registered Psychologist, and trained team coach. Declan is CEO of teamGenie®, a specialist team coaching company, and works as a top team and CEO coach.

Graham Clark is managing director of the OCM Enable, part of the OCM Group Ltd, a coaching and mentoring consultancy. He is a Chartered Occupational Psychologist and an associate fellow of the British Psychological Society. Graham has been working as a management consultant for over 20 years. His expertise covers a range of disciplines including leadership development, selecting and developing leaders, employee research and change management. He is passionate about coaching senior leaders and has worked with Board-level executives in major Global companies, as well as at the most senior levels in the UK public sector.

Dasha Grajfoner is a chartered psychologist, chartered scientist, associate fellow of the British Psychological Society (BPS) and an accredited coaching psychologist (ISCP) with a PhD in personality psychology, which she received from the University of Edinburgh. Dasha is the director of the Coachign Lab at Heriot Watt University in Edinburgh where she also lectures in coaching psychology and leadership on a Postgraduate Business Psychology Programme. Dasha is also a past chair of the Special Group in Coaching Psychology. Dasha is the author of a number of articles in coaching psychology and human–animal interactions. Her research and consultancy interests cover the application of coaching psychology in leadership and well-being and mental health improvement on one hand and animal-assisted interventions on the other.

Judit Varkonyi-Sepp is a coaching psychologist with a background in counselling, clinical and health psychology. In the last two decades she has held several leadership positions in the field of pharmaceutical and biomedical research, both in the private and public sectors. She is a registered coach for one of the large NHS Trusts in the South of England working with executives, emerging talents, organisations, businesses and individuals. Judit is a chartered scientist, a member of the British Psychological Society Special Group in Coaching Psychology, host of the Winchester area coaching psychologist peer practice group and a director of the International Society for Coaching Psychology.

Preface

It is important to update the first edition with the latest development in family business, especially during this pandemic. The guide to stimulate businesses, and to generate ideas for further development in a challenging situation is needed, and this second edition aims to provide the platform for the family business to achieve their expected business outcomes and competitive edge in their business functions using appropriate coaching interventions.

This book is written by the coaching practitioners for the coaching practitioners and the family businesses. Each author represents their leading scholarship in respective coaching practice, and their depth in knowledge and exclusive coaching experiences are eloquently presented using a practitioner's lens. The book presents the learning embedded in the coaching practices to advance coaching practices along with skills, competencies and experiences needed to provide effective coaching interventions for the family business. The use of a practitioner's lens to critically explore, discuss and analyse family business coaching practice is one of the main attraction of this book. This book is a valuable guide for the continuing professional development of coaching practitioners and businesses.

The main feature of this book is extrapolation of learning elements from the coaching practice to maintain and improve good practice in family business coaching. The critical learning issues are supported by practice-based evidence. The selected learning issues are further analysed and evaluated to facilitate good family business coaching practice by our leading practitioner authors. Each chapter is thus showcasing powerful practitioner's understanding of, and knowledge about "learning from coaching practice", and justifying the need to generate community of practice to develop a rich learning foundation for the practitioners by the practitioners.

The delivery of coaching practices using psychological principles is becoming increasingly popular in all sectors, and the learning experience inherent in a practice needs to be highlighted to demonstrate the significance in professional development and to advance coaching psychology in practice.

Despite the increasing popularity of coaching in all areas, there has not been enough attention to discuss and develop the practitioner's perspective in coaching intervention, particularly from a learning context. The key questions in this context are: what learning is embedded in a coaching intervention from a practitioner's perspective? How can coaching practices be developed using coaching practitioners' own learning experiences of the practice?

The professional developmental issue for the coaching practitioners can be addressed effectively if coaching practice is considered as a learning-focused intervention both for the coach and the coachee. The learning from the coaching practice is expected to contribute to the development of relevant skills, tools and techniques. The value of coaching practice is thus immense from a coaching practitioner's perspective: for example, a good coaching intervention can provide essential learning skills and experiences for the coaching practitioners to apply to their own practices. We have addressed these key issues of learning from coaching practices in this book.

The special feature of this book is that it is a collection of practitioners' reflective and experiential learning experiences of selected areas of family business coaching. All co-authors have applied their unique styles of presenting their arguments of learning from different areas of coaching practices. Drawing from their own practices, they have articulated key issues using relevant case studies and examples. All discussions are grounded in appropriate theoretical framework and research evidence in each chapter. We have drawn attention to the cumulative learning benefits of coaching practices to develop relevant learning-focused coaching approaches, practice-related skills and performance-based assessments.

We have explored the need for the coaching practitioners' personal and professional development using their own coaching experiences, as such, we have taken a pragmatic approach to engage practitioners to present critical appraisal of their learning from their practices.

The book has provided the platform for our co-authors to showcase their practices from a learning perspective, and to justify the need for highlighting the importance of learning from the coaching practices to enhance professional development, with particular reference to family business coaching practices. Each chapter has addressed a selected area of coaching practice and presented a selection of practical activities and tips for effective coaching practices for the family businesses. This book aims to offer arguments in favour of generating skills, tools and techniques from the learning experiences of family business coaching practices.

There is not yet any published book on coaching as a learning tool for the practitioners, particularly in a family business context, hence this book can meet the demand for professional development of coaching practitioners using their own practice-related experiences. There also appears to be a vacuum in generating ideas to develop modern, reliable and appropriate coaching application tools to serve the coaching needs of family businesses, hence this book can start the landmark to begin practitioners' journey in this area. The book is also expected to facilitate the understanding of economic growth from a family business coaching perspective, as it will provide a critical narrative of selected failures as well as successes of a few family businesses, with critical discussion on the skills generating activities for the practitioners in this context. It has thus a far-reaching goal to demonstrate the critical connections between coaching practices, business functions, experiential and reflective learning.

The major aims are:

- To provide a scholarly contribution to develop insights in the learning value of coaching practices for the practitioners.
- To present thoughtful analyses of professional initiatives to develop coaching skills from practice-related experiences, with a focus on facilitating practitioners' continuing professional development.
- To showcase the success and failure of selected case studies in order to justify the need for a family-focused approach in family business coaching.
- To appreciate the need for ongoing learning to develop good professional practices in coaching psychology using an experiential and reflective approach.

Main features

The unique features of this book are:

- Professional development of coaching practitioners with a learning-focused approach.
- Systematic and evidence-based critical discussions on effective family business coaching practice.
- Highlight of critical learning from the practice using a practitioner's lens.
- Valuable guide for continuing professional development.
- Essential compendium for family business coaching practice.
- Simple, informative and engaging language use.
- Easy to follow steps to learn and gain skills from reading each chapter.

Family business coaching is increasingly becoming a popular practice and it is not possible to capture all areas of family business coaching in a book; however, we have successfully achieved the challenge to engage our co-authors to present their reflective experiential accounts of family business practices in a few chapters. I am grateful for their valuable time, interests and contributions of selected cases from their own practices. I have achieved the benefits of collaborative learning from working with our co-authors, and it was a very pleasant learning journey. I have made a good partnership with the publisher, Routledge, and I am encouraged by their timely response, and impressed with their excellent service, which have no doubt helped me to complete the second edition of this book.

I hope this book will not only become a useful source for consultation and guidance for the coaching practitioners but also an important learning resource for the family businesses, and those interested in coaching practice, including educational institutions. Our contributions will be valuable to advance knowledge about coaching practices using an experiential and reflective approach.

Dr. Manfusa Shams, England, UK, 2021

Acknowledgements

I am very grateful to our co-authors for their contributions and interests to highlight the value of coaching practice in family businesses. I very much appreciate the support and extended co-operation from Susannah Frearson, Alexis o'Brien, and the publishing team from Routledge. I am also grateful to Prof. Stephen Palmer, Prof. Mary Watt and Dr. Ioanna Iordanou for highlighting the significance of our book in developing good coaching practices, and the practical value inherent in all chapters through their endorsement notes.

Chapter 1

Learning from family business coaching practices

Manfusa Shams

Introduction

The aim of this chapter is to present critical discussions on the nature of learning emerging from coaching family businesses. The chapter will showcase a few relevant activities to demonstrate selected areas of learning from family business coaching practices.

Drawing on the experience of delivering professional development activities for coaching psychologists and coaches, my focus is on the process of identifying the types of learning arising from coaching family businesses. The rationale for extrapolating learning elements from coaching sessions is to highlight that coaching itself is a learning process and should be integrated into academic practice.

The critical issue is how learning from the coaching practice can be used to develop relevant coaching tools and techniques. The emphasis is on coaching practitioners' engagement with the learning from the practice and developing insights in the delivery of effective coaching for family businesses.

Key questions

- What do coaching practitioners learn from their own practices?
- What types of learning are dominant from family business coaching practices?
- What is the outcome of engagement with the coaching practice from a personal learning and professional development perspective?
- What are the ethical and good professional issues in the delivery of learning from coaching?
- How do learnings from the coaching practices provide a source for shared learning for the coaching practitioners and coachees?

DOI: 10.4324/9781003174721-1

Learning from coaching practices

A brief overview of literature with a focus on learning from coaching practices indicates the absence of any direct evidence on the nature of learning from coaching family businesses. This is due to the lack of focus on coach's learning from the coaching session because attention is given to the coachee and the sessions are designed in this direction. The learning implicit in a coaching practice is thus remaining unexplored.

The discussion in this section aims to demonstrate that learning is embedded in the coaching sessions from a coaching practitioner's perspective, and that coaching practices can be further developed by the learning from the coaching sessions. This informal learning can thus provide a valuable source to apply to develop coaching practices.

There is evidence about a potential rich learning environment during the coaching sessions and the reflective practice-based learning in use to facilitate coaching practice (Grant, 2011; Turesky & Gallaghar, 2011). The key questions in this context are if there is any learning style used by coaching practitioners specifically for family business coaching? Is there any effect of the learning style on the coaching outcomes? Can we map out learning outcomes from coaching sessions?

The underlying psychological model in this context is cognitive outcomes during the coaching sessions, and their direct influences on the coaching style and social interaction with the coachees. We can use Bloom's taxonomy of cognitive outcomes approach here to represent the types of learning from a coaching session for a coaching practitioner. Anderson and Krathwohl (2001) summarised the approach in two types of dimensions: cognitive (remember, understand, apply, analyse, evaluate, create) and knowledge dimensions (propositional knowledge, procedural knowledge, metacognitive knowledge). The learning from a coaching session can be referred to as "metacognitive" knowledge as it involves pre-existing learning and new learning from the practice on a continuous basis. This is also in line with Kolb's (1984) learning cycle, and the essential feature is "learning by doing".

If the activities in a coaching session are considered as learning activities for the coach and coachees, then these activities must be aligned appropriately to the coaching outcomes to get the maximum benefits for both knowledge enhancement and performance as a coach. The alignment of learning activities with learning outcomes has been a primary focus in all types of learning (Biggs, 2003) and learning styles (Honey & Mumford, 1982). Learning is influenced by the context (Jarvela, Volet & Jarvenoja, 2010). Social and individual learning processes occur concurrently and represent distinct systemic levels (Volet, Vauras & Salonen, 2009). In the coaching context, a coach is learning from delivering coaching as well as from the interaction with the coachee and this is occurring concurrently in a coaching session. To what extent a coach can personalise the informal learning from a coaching session remains to be explored.

The critical discussion is indicating the need for coaching education incorporating the learning from the coaching sessions to provide rich, deep and focused insights in the coaching practice with a forward planning element for the coach to develop and deliver effective and appropriate coaching tools and techniques. A distinction must be drawn between coaching education and learning from the coaching sessions, and the focus in this chapter is the latter. For example, coaching education refers to formal institutionalised delivery of learning activities and resources to enhance good practice, and usually they are called "training", "professional development events", "continuing professional development", "personal development", etc. Whereas learning from the coaching session is informal, unstructured learning unless the coaching session is designed in such a way as to benefit both the coachee and the coach from a learning perspective. Vella, Crowe and Oades (2013) presented a critical analysis of coaching education and identified the dominance of a prescriptive approach in coaching education; as such, no attention is given to interpersonal competencies, personal learning and socio-cultural aspects of coaching. My discussion in this chapter is to demonstrate that informal learning from a coaching practice can be a valuable source of knowledge gaining exercise, and can also serve the purpose of formal educational experience in coaching, if the coach has the ability to identify the learning from coaching.

Drawing on the proposed concept of "critical moment" in a coaching session by Haan and Neib (2012), I will develop arguments on "critical learning" arising from critical moments during a coaching session for the coach to incorporate in their cognitive functions and social interaction with the coachee. Although critical moments during coaching can be anxiety related, leading to the termination of coaching sessions, however, a large percentage of reported critical moments are related to emerging new insights and realisations (Haan, Bertie, Day & Sills, 2010). The emerging new insights and realisations can be regarded as learning processes. A coach can have the opportunity to apply these aspects of learning from critical moments to facilitate coaching, and for use in personal and professional development. The critical learning can itself be a learning object and further exploration can bring new areas of learning from coaching. Critical learning here refers to new insights, realisations, increased understanding and novel ideas during different intervention stages of coaching. I have proposed an inventory of "critical learning" in coaching in the activity section in this chapter (Activity 1).

Areas of learning from coaching practices

Drawing from the literature, it is evident that coaching is a learning process itself independent of any other learning activities in association with coaching techniques at a particular session. The learning is informal and the coach can negotiate the learning with the coaching environment to get maximum benefits, for example, a coaching practitioner may arrange to keep a reflective diary of each coaching session to note the changes in his/her behaviour and understanding of the effectiveness of the coaching techniques, and this can form a series of informal learning segments, from which formal learning may be drawn to generate professional skills and knowledge enhancement. However, learning from a coaching session is similar to the notion of the learning combination lock (for further information, see Hartley, Woods & Pill, 2005), as the learning is drawn from a complex process of formally designed coaching session (External), and a coaching practitioner's motivation and commitment to learn from the session (Internal) including previous coaching experiences. If the combination of both external and internal factors are aligned appropriately, then we can expect the potential learning to happen for the coach. Good coaching sessions can also bring a collaborative learning experience for both the coach and a coachee. This is achieved through the dialogues between the coach and the coachee and from the discussion with other members of a family business.

There is ample evidence to suggest that informal learning can be assessed using a work-based learning approach (Eraut, 2004). However, informal learning from a coaching session is not monitored, evaluated/assessed as yet, in a family business context because any learning from coaching sessions is taken for granted, and the learner is unaware of the learning (Eraut, 2004). The learning in this context is considered as tacit knowledge; hence less attention is given to use the knowledge to deepen understanding of good coaching practices and to modify/improve the approach of family business coaching. A good plan to assess the learning from coaching can be included in the coaching intervention programme so that learning from a coaching session can be credited and recognised appropriately.

Informal learning is happening continuously without a coach's conscious awareness and efforts to learn, enriching their "educational biography" as they progress in their lifeline.

If coaching is a powerful learning tool, then it will be very important to use for personal and professional development, and the most appropriate step in this context is to capture the learning and the scope of learning from coaching practices. I have identified the following types of learning from coaching sessions:

- Formal learning
- Informal learning
- Continuous professional learning activities
- Collaborative learning
- Experiential learning
- Professional engagement
- Reflective learning
- Enquiry-based/problem-based learning.

Each of these learning types may not necessarily occur at the same time in a coaching intervention, rather there can be one particular learning type prominent in a coaching session, although both formal and informal learnings are likely to be present in a coaching intervention. An example is presented below to clarify the process of identifying a learning type in a coaching intervention with family businesses.

Example

A coaching practitioner is asked to help a family business, which is facing huge loss despite high work commitments and dedication of all family members, including good interpersonal relations and communication. The coach may use problem-based/enquiry-based learning to untie the complex knot of the business failure reasons, and at the same time learning about the key issues using this type of approach. As such, the learning emerging from this approach is grounded in problem-based/enquiry-based learning.

The process of identifying the types of learning embedded in a coaching intervention requires careful planning and designing the coaching sessions. This can also be a part of professional development in which planning and implementation of planning to achieve expected learning outcomes will be addressed.

Delivering learning from family business coaching practices

There is enough evidence to suggest that a structured coaching session can bring effective outcomes (Grant, 2011). To establish any learning from coaching family businesses, we may draw attention to the nature of coaching in this context. For example, family business coaching involves a blended approach using two parallel coaching interventions: one for the family dynamic and functions and another for business (Shams, 2011). Any learning from family businesses can be unfolded if we exploit this blended approach to establish the nature of learning embedded in family business coaching from a coaching practitioner's perspective. The learning can be how a group (family) functions and how a business operates using an evolutionary approach. Belbin's (1981) team roles can be used to learn group functions in a family context, and Tuckman and Jensen's (1977) model of group development can be used to learn about business managements, functions, operations and governance. Applying Belbin's (1981) model, the distribution of family member's roles in a business can indicate if their performances are conducive to team functions. It is expected that family members will perform to the best of their abilities if the assigned role is natural to their ability to perform in that direction. For example, if the founder of the family business is a "shaper", then this may help the other family members to accomplish their tasks using a focused approach. However, if there is no plant, then the group may lack creativity and problem-solving skills. An activity (Activity 2) is proposed to help the coaching practitioners to use Belbin's model to identify team roles in a family business and to offer effective and ethical coaching intervention. Using an integrated group function model based on both Belbin's (1981) and Tuckman and Jensen's model, it is possible to draw a functional route of a family business. For example, if a role assigned to a family member is facilitating, then the role play will be distinctive at the forming stage, in which good interpersonal relation is important to establish. Table 1.1 displays the integrated model.

This integrated family function model can be used to assess each family member's performance in relation to the assigned role. A coach will be able to detect the functional issues arising from team roles and in each stage of the family business team development. An activity to link this model in action is presented in the activity section (Activity 3). The model is a useful framework to identify the functional route of role performance for family business team development.

Table 1.1 An integrated family group function model

	Plant	Monitor evaluator	Coordinator	Resource investigator	Implementer	Complete finisher	Team worker	Shaper	Specialist
Forming									
Storming									
Norming									
Performing									
Adjourning/mourning									

Sharing learning from coaching family businesses: promoting peer practice and collaborative learning

The learning from family business coaching practices may be shared in a professional space to develop further insights in learning from coaching practice and for further professional development (Shams, 2013). Drawing from my work with coaching practitioners peer practice group, I would like to highlight the rich and deep learning benefits from group discussions and through shared ideas in selected issues in coaching psychology practice. This type of professional development platform can provide further impetus to articulate learning issues from coaching practices. It is through group learning and collaborative efforts that we will be able to develop this area of coaching psychology, that is, learning from coaching practices to develop professional coaching psychology practices. Collaborative learning (Wenger, McDermott & Snyder, 2002) from professional engagement with others can be a powerful source of knowledge-gathering exercise. This can then lead to the development of communities of practice in coaching psychology (Shams, 2013). We can apply the notion of "situated learning" (Lave & Wenger, 1991) in a coaching session to understand the learning emerging from the interaction between a coach and a coachee. The social construction of learning from a coaching intervention needs to be researched to add knowledge about the nature of learning from coaching practice, and how a coach can be benefitted from learning from the practice as a part of their professional development. Social media has an important role to develop collaborative learning from coaching practices, along with the use of a personal reflective diary/journal to record learning from each coaching session.

Family business coaching practitioners' initiatives to develop a professional group to facilitate discussions around good and ethical practices in family businesses in the UK can make an important contribution to develop coaching psychology. As family businesses are contributing a high percentage to the national economy around the world, it is important to deliver family business coaching as an important subject area in the higher educational institutions. This will then help to build up knowledge and understanding of the psychology of family business from a coaching context. It is interesting to note that although coaching psychology is now formally delivered by a number of UK universities and higher education institutions, however, family business coaching is not included in the curriculum. The exclusion of this area demands attention from academics and practitioners to deliver an inclusive coaching psychology programme in the higher educational institutions.

Activities and assessments

Activity 1: inventory of critical learning

Instruction

This inventory aims to record the occurrence of "critical learning" during different coaching intervention stages.

Please put a tick against each area of your critical learning (new insights, realisations, increased understanding, innovative ideas) at different points of the timeline in a coaching intervention.

Analysis

Draw a graph indicating the stage point where your learning is higher than at any other stage point. This may then help you to understand how you can engage with learning at that stage taking a focused approach.

Table 1.2 Inventory of critical learning

Coaching timeline	New insights	Realisations	Increased understanding	Innovative ideas
Beginning				
Middle				
End				
After-end				

Activity 2: placing family members in different team roles

Instruction

Obtain information on each member's role in a family business using the nine categories below. Place each member of a family business (family and non-family) in the role category to assess their performances.

Table 1.3 Placing family members in different team role

	Plant	Monitor evaluator	Coordinator	Resource investigator	Implementer	Complete finisher	Teamworker	Shaper	Specialist
Father									
Mother									
Sons									
Daughters									
Uncle									
Auntie									
Niece/Nephew									
Nonfamily member									
Other—specify									

Activity 3: functional route to family business teamwork

Instruction

The following model can help a coach to identify the role performance of each family member in relation to family business team development. For each stage of the team development on the left side of the table (forming, storming, norming, performing and adjourning), please indicate the involvement of each role.

Table 1.4(a) Functional route to family business teamwork

	Plant	Monitor evaluator	Coordinator	Resource investigator	Implementer	Complete finisher	Team worker	Shaper	Specialist
Forming									
Storming									
Norming									
Performing									
Adjourning/mourning									

Learning outcomes

It is expected that at the end of this assessment, a coach will be able to develop a functional route for each family member to develop family business team-work. The functional route will help the coach to identify any dysfunctions in the role performance affecting the team development.

A completed example of an integrated family group function model can be seen in Table 1.4(b).

Table 1.4(b) A completed example: functional route to family business teamwork

	Plant	Monitor evaluator	Coordinator	Resource investigator	Implementer	Complete Finisher	Team worker	Shaper	Specialist
Forming	✓								
Storming		✓			✓				
Norming			✓			✓		✓	
Performing			✓	✓			✓		
Adjourning/mourning							✓		✓

Tips for learning from your practices

Can you apply a "practice what we preach" concept in your coaching practice?

Below are a few major tips for you to learn from your coaching practice:

1   Draw a list of intended learning outcomes from each coaching session.
2   Keep a record of what you have learnt in each session and at what stage.
3   Evaluate your learning experience in each session using this five-point scale:

Good—Adequate—Same as before—Little learning—No learning.

4   Relate new learning to any previous learning to develop a reflective journal.
5   Monitor your progress to develop new learning using a peer supervision approach.
6   Explore the possibility of developing new techniques and tools from the new learning to apply to your coaching practice and for the wide application.

Conclusion

Coaching can provide a rich learning environment for the coach to increase their cognitive functions and social aspects of learning. The learning inherent in a coaching session usually remains unexplored due to the lack of awareness of learning emerging from the coaching practice. This is also due to attention paid primarily to the coachee; as such, the learning needs of the coach are not taken into consideration at the time of coaching intervention. However, informal learning occurring naturally from the coaching practice can provide very useful knowledge to enhance good practice with ethical consideration appropriately. The learning in this context is called "metacognitive" knowledge because of the blend of new knowledge with the existing knowledge. If the learning objective from the coaching sessions can be aligned with the approach of coaching and assessment of the coaching outcome, then a coaching practice will bring an equal level of benefits for both a coach and a coachee. There is hardly any research attention in this area, and I have argued for increasing awareness of the benefits of learning from the coaching sessions for a coach to develop professional skills. Although the nature of learning is not yet established through empirical research, however, the informal learning embedded in coaching sessions can stimulate further development and insights in delivering effective coaching intervention.

References

Anderson, L. W., & Krathwohl, D. R. (2001). *A Taxonomy for Learning, Teaching and Assessment*. New York, NY: Addison Wesley Longman.

Belbin, R. M. (1981). *Management Teams: Why They Succeed or Fail*. Oxford, UK: Butterworth-Heinemann.

Biggs, J. (2003). *Teaching for Quality Learning at University* (2nd ed.). Buckingham: Society for Research in Higher Education and Open University Press.

Eraut, M. (2004). Informal learning in the workplace. *Studies in Continuing Education, 26*: 247–273.

Grant, M. A. (2011). Is it time to REGROW the GROW model? Issues related to teaching coaching session structures. *The Coaching Psychologist, 7*: 118–126.

Haan, D. E., Bertie, C., Day, A., & Sills, C. (2010). Critical moments of clients and coaches: A direct-comparison study. *International Coaching Psychology Review, 5*: 109–128.

Haan, D. E., & Neib, C. (2012). Critical moments in a coaching case study: Illustrations of a process research model. *Consulting Psychology Journal: Practice and Research, 64*: 198–224.

Hartley, P., Woods, A., & Pill, M. (2005). *Enhancing Teaching in Higher Education*. London: Kogan Page.

Honey, P., & Mumford, A. (1982). *The Manual of Learning Styles*. Maiden-head, England: Peter Honey Publication.

Jarvela, S., Volet, S., & Jarvenoja, H. (2010). Research on motivation in collaborative learning: Moving beyond the cognitive–situative divide and combining individual and social processes. *Educational Psychologist, 45*(1): 15–27.

Kolb, D. A. (1984). *Experiential Learning*. New Jersey, NJ: Prentice-Hall, Englewood Cliffs.

Lave, J., & Wenger, E. (1991). *Situated Learning: Legitimate Peripheral Participation*. Cambridge, UK: Cambridge University Press.

Shams, M. (2011). Recent developments in family business coaching. In: M. Shams & D. Lane (Eds.), *Coaching in the Family Owned Business: A Path to Growth* (pp. 13–20). London: Routledge.

Shams, M. (2013). Communities of coaching practice: Developing a new approach. *International Coaching Psychology Review, 8*: 89–91.

Tuckman, B., & Jensen, M. (1977). Stages of small-group development revisited. *Group and Organisational Studies, 2*: 419–427.

Turesky, F. E., & Gallaghar, D. (2011). Know thyself: Coaching for leadership using Kolb's experiential learning theory. *The Coaching Psychologist, 7*(1): 5–14.

Vella, A. S., Crowe, P. T., & Oades, G. L. (2013). Increasing the effectiveness of formal coach education: Evidence of a parallel process. *International Journal of Sports Science & Coaching, 8*: 417–430.

Volet, S. E., Vauras, M., & Salonen, P. (2009). Self-and social regulation in learning contexts: An integrative perspective. *Educational Psychologist, 44*: 215–226.

Wenger, E., McDermott, R., & Snyder, W. M. (2002). *Cultivating Communities of Practice*. Boston, MA: Harvard Business School Press.

Chapter 2

Family business coaching
A practitioner's perspective

Manfusa Shams and Janey Howl

Introduction

The effective delivery of family business coaching requires a good understanding of the infrastructure of family businesses and an appreciation of learning needs for the development of skills specific to delivering family business coaching, including relevant ethical issues (Shams, 2006). As family businesses can be reluctant to disclose information about internal business functions due to privacy and competition with other entrepreneurs, there can also be resistance to a coaching intervention. A coach should be professionally competent to deal with potential resistance, hostility and intolerance from any family member during the period of coaching intervention. Knowledge about integrated coaching techniques with a focus on diversifying skills to address relevant coaching needs, combined with a sensitive approach to addressing family functions in relation to business functions and vice versa, will ensure good and ethical practice to deliver effective coaching for a family business. The alignment issues between families and businesses are yet to be fully discussed in the literature. There is a need to document practitioners' experience of family business coaching to develop coaching practice and related tools and techniques. The insights drawn by the practitioners from their practices can provide a rich source of resources to apply to advance and facilitate effective coaching intervention for family businesses. A good practice is always informed by relevant knowledge and the application of the knowledge to a practical setting, such as family business coaching (Shams, 2011a).

In this chapter, we will address the following key questions.

Key questions

- What are the critical issues in family dynamics affecting business functions?
- What should be done to align family with business in a coaching intervention?

DOI: 10.4324/9781003174721-2

- Why should family business coaching address the interdependency between families and their businesses?
- What practice is in place to develop non-family members in a family-owned business?
- What major behavioural and emotional issues need to be included in coaching a family-owned business?
- How can a good understanding of the interplay between family and business help develop professional skills in coaching practice?
- How can an understanding of family business coaching advance the knowledge of coaching psychology as a practice-based discipline?

Understanding family dynamics: practice-related issues

The coach is stepping into a complex system, where things are rarely what they seem, and loyalties and resentments run deep. The coach to a family business is contracting with individuals, with the family and with the business entity. It is vital to distinguish three separate components of working within a family business: family issues, business ownership issues, and issues of running a business. All three sets of issues are complex systems in their own right. The contracting process must clearly articulate professional boundaries, personal and professional integrity, confidentiality, legal obligations, and how potential conflicts of interest and ethical dilemmas that may emerge will be handled. In eighty five per cent of cases known to the authors where coaching interventions in family businesses have had a bad outcome (for either the coach or the business), failures can be related to weak contracting.

The professional outsider is engaged to bring objectivity, but over time may, to a degree, become part of the family and should be prepared for the reality that coaching in a family business is likely to surface personal baggage. In a business where the family is divided, the coach may experience feelings of conflicting loyalties, and must take positive action to avoid the pitfalls of collusion, and becoming yet another player in the family game. The coach requires intellectual rigour, emotional robustness, the integrity to handle their own "stuff" and strong supervision. Successful engagement depends upon rigour in contracting at the outset, starting with the end in mind and with the end clearly defined. Family businesses are notorious for either finding it hard to part with trusted advisors or choosing to shoot the messenger. Keep the exit strategy firmly in view, testing it regularly and rigorously.

Case study 1

Amelie, a highly experienced coach, was engaged to develop the Board of a family owned retail chain. The five directors spanned three generations. Trust, liking, and respect were mutual from the outset. Amelie was careful to respect professional boundaries and resisted the temptation to accept invitations to family events. In the second year of engagement it became apparent that the sales director, the CEO's daughter, was not upping her game and her inability to enhance performance was limiting business growth. Naming the "elephant in the room" was difficult but necessary and the whole family recognised the truth and thanked Amelie for her courage and integrity. However, behind the scenes over the course of a single weekend, the family closed ranks; the sales director resorted to tears, tantrums, and emotional manipulation. Amelie's contract was terminated, with significant regret, by the CEO on Monday morning.

All coaches who work with powerful decision makers run the risk of being a victim of their success whenever they cross paths with senior influencers who lack integrity. However, playing politics in a corporate, as opposed to a family, environment is usually more covert, and lower risk. As Amelie learnt the hard way, "Never forget that blood is always thicker than water. You're incredibly vulnerable in a family business, and sometimes the bad guys win". What would she do differently? Amelie now always partners with a colleague because although the size of the assignment may not justify it, the inherent complexity of a family business does.

Interdependency between families and their businesses

Conflict and relationships are significant coaching areas for family businesses. Typically, conflict is either completely suppressed, as in "Oh, we all get on really well … Of course we are all agreed on strategy", or it is open warfare to the point where some family members will refuse to be in the same room. In order to make an effective coaching intervention, it is important to understand the powerful dynamic of kinship in managing, developing and operating a family business. Nicholson (2008) has used evolutionary theory to underpin the influence of kinship in family business functions.

Family business is truly personal, so the coach is rarely just coaching the business or indeed the person/people in the room. Shadow elements within the family can be toxic, as spouses, children's children, cousins and other disparate members fuel fires of mistrust, disagreement and entitlement. Furthermore, issues of marital strife, separation or divorce and the acquisition of new spouses and children have a huge impact on financial and succession planning for family businesses.

The ultimate coaching challenge is usually equipping clients to engage in respectful relationships and healthy conflict. There will be a focus on relationship first and outcomes second; on respecting self and others; on improving standards of behaviour; on mapping stakeholder relationships and increasing circles of influence. Conflict becomes the respectful kind that stimulates genuine curiosity, innovation and business growth. Along the way, the coach can expect to facilitate various crucial conversations, surfacing long held and sometimes hidden resentments, as family members learn to align around business strategy.

A family business represents a complex interplay between family and business matters, as shown in Figure 2.1.

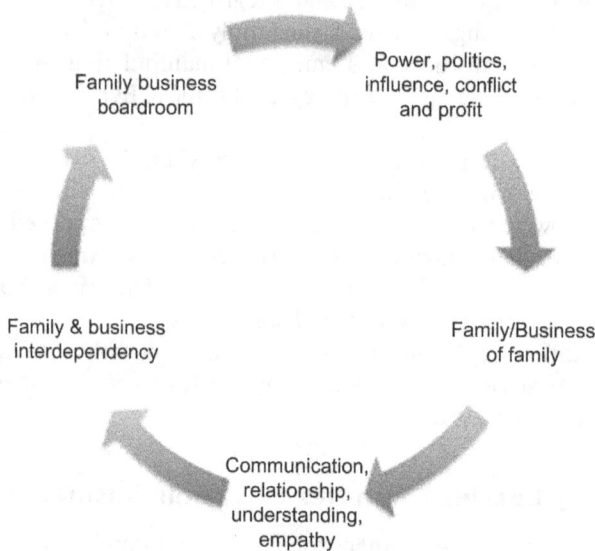

Figure 2.1 Family business boardroom: functional capabilities.

This is leading to a blended function by the family for the family business, in which family business board room may become a family discussion room, and power, family politics, conflict, communication, relationship, finance and profit all merged to either provide an integrated family business or a crisis to separate out family issues from business functions. Boundaries between family and business issues are frequently blurred. The successful interface between power, family politics, conflict, communication, relationship, finance and profit can create an integrated family business. A failure to integrate these dynamics usually results in a crisis of some description (Figure 2.1). A crisis in a family business is illustrated in the case study below.

Case study 2

Consider Richard's client, a niche diamond business. David the charismatic founder, CEO, and internationally renowned expert in his field, was as demanding of his staff as of himself. His wife, Sarah, combined her role of finance director with that of PA to her husband. The other key player—David's younger brother Lloyd—was given the title of commercial director.

He handled everything not controlled by his brother and sister-in-law. Richard was called in at crisis point: staff morale and family bickering had hit an all-time low, and despite commercial success and increasing client demand, the business was in danger of imploding.

Richard won the trust of all parties, quickly uncovering a mass of anger and emotional baggage. Sarah was financial director, despite limited qualifications and aptitude, because the brothers wanted "to keep business in the family". Sarah was PA because she did not trust her husband; by controlling his diary and travel bookings she believed she could "keep tabs on him". Coaching revealed Sarah's deep-seated resentments towards her husband and allegations of "bullying". Lloyd blamed the high staff turnover and bad office atmosphere on Sarah. Richard established clear rules of conduct, but these were undermined by explosive outbursts at home. The marriage was under severe threat. The business was highly dysfunctional. Richard referred Sarah for therapy, recognising that dealing with her toxicity and victim mentality were beyond his expertise, and critical to a successful business outcome. Richard helped the team to redefine roles and accountabilities based on personal competences and to recruit additional professional staff.

Richard's successful intervention was the result of the application of many years of professional expertise in the development of people and organisations. His business knowledge and expertise in psychometrics enabled him to realign strategic direction and to define roles and responsibilities. Richard's coaching expertise was crucial in addressing toxic relationships, establishing personal and professional boundaries, and in identifying when additional support was necessary; in this case a therapeutic intervention. His personal integrity won—and maintained—the trust of all parties, giving him the courage to challenge when people stepped out of line and to tell the truth as he saw it.

Supporting non-family leaders in a family business

Coaching the non-family leader of a family business is not dissimilar to coaching any corporate executive. There are, however, three distinct areas of specific challenge which non-family leaders face over and over again: innovation, leadership and managing performance.

a) Innovation

Decisions on innovation in a family-owned business are frequently based on a personal whim, rather than on rigorous market research and analysis. The emotional bias cuts both ways; sometimes against, and sometimes in favour of, innovation, with the consequence that change can happen instantly, incredibly slowly or not at all.

Case study 3

Ted, for example, is finance and operations director (dual roles frequently go with the territory) of a successful family-owned publishing business, an industry whose survival depends on mastery of the digital knowledge economy. He faced strong resistance to change from the family. Coaching uncovered that what he experienced as a mass resistance was in fact an aggregate of individual resistances with various root causes: some were based on a closed mindset; some were due to fear of the unknown and for some family members it was simply about timeline for return on investment, because they had personal financially ambitious exit strategies. Resistance to change tends to be amplified within what may be viewed as a heritage business, such as publishing, but all family businesses have a significant legacy component.

Case study 4

When two young family members joined the board of a textile manufacturing business, Sam's challenge was to slow down innovation. The next generation wanted to indulge personal passions for technology, social media, travel, and property by driving through diversification, and venturing into emerging markets; rapid change that did not enhance the current brand.

b) Leadership

What does it mean to run a business with full accountability, but lack of autonomy? Personal whim is a recurring theme in coaching non-family leaders in particular, and in family-run businesses in general. Mainly David is left to run the business but has, on occasion, to deal with the fallout of his maverick founder's personal passions and prejudices. A single call from the iconic founder pulled the plug on a significant merger deal.

> Telling the troops was really hard. They'd burned the midnight oil for months … and worse it had a massive negative impact on bonus. And what do I tell them? That it's off because he [the founder] has a personal vendetta from twenty years ago with one of the key players?

David did tell his people that. What he did not share was his suspicion that the whole aborted venture had been the founder's calculated act of revenge on former business adversaries.

c) Managing performance

Managing performance—one's own and that of other people—is always prime coaching territory. It is particularly nuanced for non-family leaders, where the fundamental criterion for board membership is bloodline, rather than skill and competence. In a context where business is most definitely personal, it is easy to appreciate why feedback is perceived as just too difficult.

And yet feedback is critical for adjusting behaviour, and for monitoring and achieving outcomes. Although usually well rewarded financially, the non-family leader often struggles to get meaningful feedback on his or her own performance independently of business results. The coach adds huge value by helping the client to determine own goals, benchmark externally, and to evaluate process as well as outcomes. Initiating a 360-degree feedback process with non-family leaders can often be the leverage to initiate a feedback and performance culture within the family.

How to coach non-family leaders?

In parallel to working on innovation, leadership, and managing performance, a non-family leader appreciates other specific coaching interventions that reflect the unique nature of the role. Suggestions for development include work on the leadership context in its entirety, and connectedness in terms of building a strong support community beyond the "family". Furthermore, no intervention can be complete without work on power, profit and politics, the lifeblood of any business and of particular significance in family owned businesses.

a) Create a context

It is important to help your client understand the wider context of their role within a family business, as a reference point for self-awareness and on-going development.

Traditional models of leadership do not fully reflect the somewhat special circumstances of non-family leaders. Elements of models of stewardship and servant leadership usually resonate profoundly with non-family leaders, as capturing the reality of their business world. Share and explore with your client. The co-creation of a relevant conceptual framework provides a strong coaching foundation for both client and coach.

b) Build connectedness

Being a non-family leader in a family controlled business is frequently experienced as a lonely place. It is important to coach your client to build a professional community.

Case study 5

As General Counsel to an international family-owned retail empire, Emily frequently flies into a beautiful tax haven to attend meeting at the luxurious family estate where several generations of the family work and play. "It sounds glamorous but I arrive alone and leave on my own. It's their DNA, their dynasty, but in the end it's just my day job".

Work with your client to form a strong support team, both professional and personal, outside the family business, including mentors and colleagues from varied industry sectors. Encourage your client to build a strong social community, and to commit to leisure interests. Otherwise the non-family business leader risks isolation, and loss of perspective.

c) Coach the 3 Ps

Family owned businesses are a heady mix of "Power, Profit and Politics". It is important to work with your client on developing an awareness of the complex interplay of all three. Remind your client that power is always personal. Focus on purpose behind profit. Coach your client on putting people before politics.

Power = Personal

In a family owned business, the power lies with the family; everything is personal and will be taken personally. Coach your client to achieve extraordinary levels of diplomacy.

Purpose beyond profit

Purpose varies according to an individual family member's specific interests. Coach your client to recognise and leverage different purposes.

People before politics

Non-family leaders often spend a significant amount of time "managing" the family stakeholders. Coach your client to move beyond politics and focus on the people in the business.

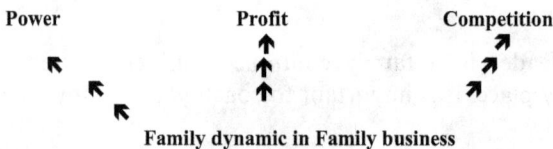

Power   Profit   Competition

Family dynamic in Family business

Figure 2.2 Family business is influenced by family politics, power and profit.

Behavioural and emotional issues

Overstressed family business owners juggling office and personal life often have no boundary between work and home. When business is going badly, there is no respite, no safe place. It takes its toll on physical health and emotional well-being. The risk of burnout is high, as exhaustion and friction replace passion and purpose. Symptoms include temper tantrums and/or tears, rudeness, lack of self-care, unfeasibly long hours, poor-quality decision-making, "stuckness", busyness rather than productivity, and complaints of "It's not fair".

The coach's goal is to take toxic emotion out of the business, leaving heart and passion. Supporting family members to let go of past resentments is vital. The focus is on wellness, both for individuals and the collective. There are two immediate areas for coaches to address: building resilience and creating boundaries. Work in these areas reaps immediate benefits for all concerned, establishing trust in the process, the coach, each other and individual capacity to learn and grow. The uniquely contagious nature of family-owned business represents both challenge and opportunity: bad behaviour spreads like wildfire, but then so does good.

a) Resilience

It is recommended that initial work on building resilience focuses on both a physical component and a mental component. The client and coach will choose the single physical change that will be a quick win and create energy, belief and a firm foundation for the work to come. Typical examples include exercise, sleep patterns, simple dietary changes, drinking more water, connecting with nature and taking time out to rest or play.

All coaches have their favoured approaches to building mental resilience, and every client circumstance is of course unique. Mindfulness and gratitude may be neither the easiest nor the most obvious place to begin but they come highly recommended. Family businesses are accompanied by baggage, frequently with a past that is emotionally bigger than the present or future. In support of whatever systemic interventions the coach is making, the coach will reap dividends by encouraging each client to experiment and develop their own mindfulness and gratitude practices. Sharing and learning from different experiences helps members to see themselves and each other in a different light and to pay attention to creating a shared future.

b) Mindfulness and gratitude

Family members will choose different mindfulness practices, and individuals and the business will benefit from the enhanced clarity of thought and better quality decision-making that all mindfulness practice engenders.

It is human nature to notice what we lack rather than to celebrate our abundance; to look at how far we have to travel rather than how far we have come; to clock the failures and not the wins. An attitude of gratitude always works wonders. The benefits in a family business are manifold as daily gratitude practice will usually result in a greater appreciation of each other: colleagues are, after all, family.

c) Boundaries

Handling tolerations is a particularly good place to start in coaching within a family business as many tolerations are amplified because they are shared, particularly where people both live and work together. It is helpful for each individual to make two top ten lists of stuff they are tolerating: one for work and one for home. Strategise pooling resources to eradicate tolerations with particular emphasis on easy wins and those tolerations that are shared by more than one person.

Developing family business coaching practice

The coach's introduction to family business coaching may be through coaching a single individual, or facilitating a team within the business, or it could be a larger organisational intervention. The family-owned business in terms of size may sit anywhere on the SME spectrum, or may indeed be a large corporate. The nature of coaching in smaller family businesses is that whatever the initial entry point, the assignment frequently grows exponentially as trust and confidence in the coach grows and the history and complexity of family interaction unfolds. The following tip box is offered as a guide to support both new and experienced coaches in their work with family businesses.

Top tips for coaching a family-owned business: are you ready?

- Do you have real mastery of all fundamental coaching skills?
- How well do you apply them to working with interrelated groups of different sizes and functions?
- How well do you understand complex systems? What models can you reference? What experience can you draw upon?
- How do you demonstrate and maintain integrity in complex spaces?
- What training, background and experience do you have in relational dynamics, for example, transactional analysis, psychotherapy, gestalt, psychology, counselling?
- What are your arrangements for professional supervision?
- How much professional indemnity insurance cover do you have?
- What records do you keep? What are the legal implications regarding data protection?

Answer: You have been warned! In an area where angels fear to tread, great coaching skills and personal integrity are not enough. Increase your skills and knowledge, and up your supervision, in the certain knowledge that coaching in a family business is intellectually, professionally and emotionally demanding.

Toolkit—top ten for coaching a family-owned business

It is recommended that the coach has expertise in four areas: coaching methodology, psychological measurement, life tools and organisational tools. In terms of coaching methodology, a robust philosophy is required to set standards, withhold scrutiny and maintain the personal and professional integrity of all parties. Psychological measurement is essential to provide objectivity and a shared frame of reference. Life tools are a valuable resource in developing the heart of a family business, and organisational tools provide a meaningful framework for business development. The specific tool in each area is a matter of personal choice, and the following suggestions are recommendations, not prescriptions.

Table 2.1 Toolkit – top ten for coaching a family-owned business

Coaching methodology	Life tools	Organisational tools	Psychological measurement
Appreciative enquiry	Life wheel	Personal development plan	Personality type
Solution focused	Digital technology applications	Values, vision and mission	360-degree feedback instrument
Clean language			Emotional intelligence

Placing family business coaching in coaching psychology

The discussion in this chapter has argued for the development of family business coaching using psychological models, theories and relevant practice-related issues.

Family business coaching practice is still underdeveloped from a psychological perspective. This is because of the complex nature of coaching in this context, as it requires a blended coaching approach to address the needs of a family and their businesses (Shams, 2011b). Furthermore, the contributions of multiple disciplines have added further complexity. It is difficult to isolate the significant psychological models, theories and evidence-based critical discussions (Haan & Duckworth, 2012) that have contributed to an understanding of family business coaching. For example, sports coaches, psychotherapists, counsellors, family therapists and business executives are all involved in coaching.

Although their focuses and approaches may be different, they evidence good success rates for the delivery of coaching interventions addressing specific issues. The key issue here is to identify the application of techniques and tools embedded in the discipline of psychology, so that the major contributions from psychology can be highlighted and developed further to promote family business coaching in coaching psychology.

Table 2.2 Descriptions of top ten toolkits for family business coaching

Coaching methodology	Life tools	Organisational tools	Psychological measurement
Appreciative enquiry	Life wheel	Personal development plan	Personality type

A consulting technique that builds businesses around what works, rather than trying to fix what does not.
  It utilises the cycle of DISCOVER_DREAM_ DESIGN_DESTINY to focus business development.
	A fundamental coaching tool for assessing the quality of various aspects of the human experience, essential for well-being.
	  It is a powerful diagnostic for coaching family members.
	  Areas typically covered include career/profession, vitality, family/ parenting, relationships, fun/enjoyment, personal finance, personal development and spiritual awareness.
		A personal development plan (PDP) process that drives business excellence is key to establishing progression towards measurable business outcomes.
		  PDPs will typically be designed to develop both strengths and weaknesses, and involve elements of coaching and reflection.
		  They will be evidence-based, drawing upon self-awareness, feedback, values and goal-setting.
			A type-based psychometric, such as the Myers–Briggs Type Indicator, provides a framework for personal and team development.
			  It helps family members to understand and appreciate qualitative differences between individuals and supports them in developing more effective communication and influencing skills.
			  A type-based psychometric is particularly helpful in coaching situations that demand skills in handling conflict or conducting difficult conversations.

Table 2.2 Cont.

Coaching methodology	Life tools	Organisational tools	Psychological measurement
Solution focused	Applications— digital technology	Values, vision and mission	360-degree feedback instrument
A consulting technique that affirms collaborative, personalised, strength-based values.	There are a plethora of apps, many of them free, and all available 24/7, to support the client in personal development.	Values, vision and mission are the heartbeat of the business. They drive strategy and ethics, they define brand and identity, and they inform communication, policy and relationships.	Multi-rater feedback effectively benchmarks personal and organisational performance.
Its emphasis on simplicity, economical use of resources and a clear focus on sustainable outcomes makes it a particularly valuable intervention with family businesses.	They address multiple aspects of personal and business life. They help users set and achieve goals; use reinforcement to create new habits; and provide public accountability and communities of support.		It provides objective metrics against which to measure development. An instrument that incorporates both qualitative and quantitative data is recommended.
Clean language			Emotional intelligence
A questioning and discussion technique that enables people to convey their own meaning. It provides freedom from the emotional spin, bias and prejudice of others, making it a particularly valuable technique in the family business setting.			Work on emotional intelligence will improve family relationships in private life, as well as in the business.

(continued)

Table 2.2 Cont.

Coaching methodology	Life tools	Organisational tools	Psychological measurement
			Practitioners are advised to select a robust tool that identifies emotional competencies as learned capabilities, rather than innate talents. Successful application will promote the achievement of outstanding business performance.

The leading question in this context is why is it important to place family business coaching in coaching psychology?

Family businesses are contributing a significantly high percentage to national economy (Shams & Lane, 2011). Ensuring the sustained growth of family businesses can help to increase the national economy from this sector. Coaching psychologists can make a major contribution to provide support to family businesses. Systematic exploration of family dynamics in a business context can provide significant insights into the psychological processes of family functions and the intertwined coaching approach. Family business coaching thus can help unpack the complexities in the delivery of relevant psychological theories and models from a family-centred perspective, with the prospect of enhancing knowledge and understanding about the benefits of psychological approaches to address coaching needs for a family business.

The appropriate documentation of a coach and a coaching practitioner's rich experience in family business coaching needs to be affirmed using a collective approach and efforts to advance forward thinking and planning in this area. The maturity of coaching psychology as a distinctive discipline depends on the development of different areas of coaching, and family business coaching is one such area with good prospects of making significant contributions. Drawing from their unique experiences to coach family businesses, coaching practitioners/psychologists can help develop the discipline, with a focus on the applications of psychological models, theories and evidence, so that the value of psychological knowledge to family business coaching can be recognised appropriately.

Family business coaching can usefully be viewed as a specific genre in the coaching psychology canon, with considerable potential to add new knowledge to the discipline. Many coaching psychologists and consultants have direct experience as employees or owners of family businesses, and an increasing number are choosing to specialise in working with such entities. Direct experience is an asset that enhances credibility, but it is, by no means, a prerequisite.

The diversity of family businesses—particularly in terms of size, global reach and degree of "corporateness"—presents a challenge for coaching psychology as a profession in terms of training, developing and supporting skilled practitioners. There is no simple "one size fits all" model. However, what is clear is that family business presents a potential minefield for the unwary; between the long tail of history and the creation of legacy is space in which coaching practitioners make professional interventions with far-reaching consequences. They require expertise in the core disciplines of coaching psychology, considerable experience of working with individuals and businesses, an extensive professional toolkit, excellent supervision, exemplary integrity, personal resilience and considerable mental agility.

Conclusion

In this chapter, we have presented our critical and thoughtful analysis of good practice in coaching family businesses from a practitioner's perspective. Our focus was the effective delivery of coaching using a family-centred approach for family businesses. The chapter has highlighted important coaching practice-related issues to draw attention to coaches and coaching psychologists to develop their practice using the practical suggestions, top ten toolkits and coaching techniques appropriate to coach all involved in a family business, including non-family members.

The discussion has justified that family business coaching can be an area of practice for coaching psychologists using psychological models, theories and relevant evidence.

As evident in our discussion, family business coaching is built upon the psychological models, theories and evidence-based findings of coaching psychology. Family businesses derive huge benefit from the skilled application of coaching psychology, and as practitioners we are committed to making excellent professional interventions and sharing best practice. Collaboration is the route via which we will build our theoretical frameworks, increase the knowledge bank of our discipline, enhance our ability to service our clients and ultimately grow the considerable wealth and opportunities that are created by family businesses for the benefit of the economy and society as a whole.

References

Haan, De. E., & Duckworth, A. (2012). Signalling a new trend in executive coaching outcome research. *International Coaching Psychology Review, 8*(1): 6–19.

Nicholson, N. (2008). Evolutionary psychology and family business: A new synthesis for theory, research, and practice. *Family Business Review, 21*(1): 103–118.

Shams, M. (2006). Approaches in business coaching: Exploring context-specific and cultural issues. In: M. Shams & P. Jackson (Eds.), *Developments in Work and Organizational Psychology: Implications for International Business* (pp. 228–244). The Netherlands: Elsevier.

Shams, M. (2011a). Recent developments in family business coaching. In: M. Shams & D. Lane (Eds.), *Coaching in the Family Owned Business: A Path to Growth* (pp. 13–20). London: Routledge.

Shams, M. (2011b). Key issues in family business coaching. In: M. Shams & D. Lane (Eds.), *Coaching in the Family Owned Business: A Path to Growth* (pp. 1–12). London: Karnac.

Shams, M., & Lane, D. (2011). *Coaching in the Family Owned Business: A Path to Growth*. London: Karnac.

Chapter 3

Developing family business coaching using a family-centred approach

Manfusa Shams

Introduction

The voluminous literature of family business has offered a number of theoretical explanations for the way a family business is functioning and the strong influence of family functions per se on the family business (Shams, 2011). Family business is characterised as a unique economic organisation for the pattern of ownership, governance, management and succession, influencing the organisation's goals, structure and functional strategies to transfer succession power to the next generation (Chua, Chrisman & Sharma, 1999).

The reciprocal influence of family functions on business and business functions on family has been documented, and the inseparable bond between a family and their business is highlighted in the literature (Olson et al., 2003; Shams, 2011). Despite the voluminous literature, there is hardly any published work on coaching family businesses using a family-centred approach.

This chapter aims to present a set of activities to extrapolate the key issues of a family-centred approach for family business coaching practitioners. It is expected that the activities will provide the ideas to develop relevant tools and techniques to develop a family-centred coaching approach for family businesses. The activities are based on relevant psychological principles and theories, and they can be used as a resource for future research in family business coaching.

Key questions

- What is a family-centred approach in relation to family business coaching?
- How a family-centred approach can be applied to enhance good practice for family business coaching?
- What are the ethical and professional issues in a family-centred approach?
- How a family-centred coaching approach can be developed using relevant tools and techniques?

DOI: 10.4324/9781003174721-3

What is a family-centred approach?

A family-centred approach places family first in the intervention process; as such, issues relating to family functions dominate the coaching practices. A recent development in the literature is the attention to family coaching as a part of the development of family science, as such, a family-centred coaching is obviously addressing family issues independent of any business-related issues, with an aim to help families to function effectively (Allen & Huff, 2014). The focus in this context is to increase capabilities and skills of family members to develop as a functional unit (Rush, Shelden & Hanft, 2003). A family-centred coaching approach is also a favourite option for many families for consultation relating to family matters in addition to business coaching (Baker & Allen, 2014). Family coaching is developed from family life, education and coaching psychology (Allen, 2013); hence, a family-centred approach in coaching family business is essential to achieve successful outcomes for the family.

If a business is performed using family members mainly, then we must consider the importance of applying a family-centred approach. The context in which a family business operates has a significant influence on the governance, operation and performance of the business; hence, business originating from a family must consider the family as a context to develop and design an appropriate coaching intervention. The question is how can we develop an appropriate coaching intervention taking a family as a context? A family-centred approach using relevant techniques and tools can address this question. One such approach is the application of structural and relational dynamics in a family to address specific business-related issues in a coaching practice. An outline of this approach along with a graphical representation is presented in the next section.

Application of a family-centred approach

A family business determines the nature and goal of their business. With diverse family systems in different cultural contexts, we must explore the most effective way to deliver any coaching intervention to maximise the benefits of the intervention for a family business. A family-centred approach can satisfy the need for meeting the needs of family businesses irrespective of cultural context, family and business types (Shams, 2006).

Research evidence indicates three streams of attitudes in relation to family business across Asia and America, and these are "the family in", "the family out" and "the family-business jugglers" (Birley, 2001). The "family in" attitude asserts the definite entry of family members into the business, confirming the generational succession pathway, but the "the family out" and "the family-business jugglers" remain indecisive to enter the family business. The "family in" attitude is more prominent in the Asian countries (e.g. India, Japan) and the "family out" and "family-business jugglers" are more predominant in the American context. A family-centred approach must take into consideration of these differential attitudinal issues in the intervention.

An activity is proposed below to demonstrate a family-centred approach that can be used in all contexts and may be regarded as a value-free technique.

Activity 1: A family-centred approach

Table 3.1

Family type	No. of family members	Role in the business	Family structure and relationship	Communication style and cohesion

Introduction to a family →coaching begins →family roles in business→communication→relationships→expectations and goal-setting→coaching techniques, tools identified→coaching delivered.

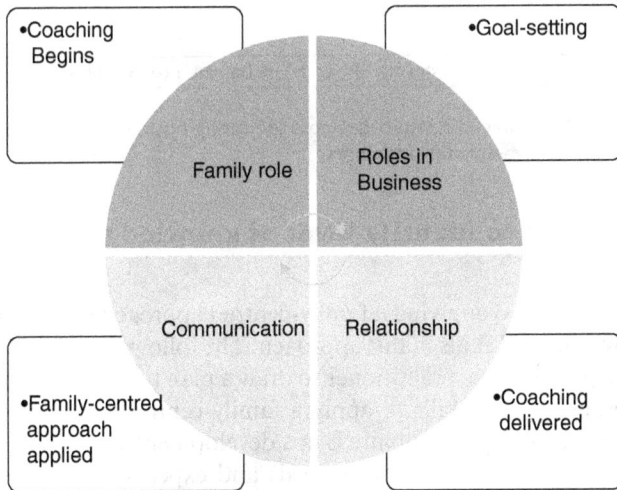

Figure 3.1 Stages in the application of a family-centred approach in coaching a family business.

Activity 2: An example of a family-centred approach in coaching practice

A travel agency owned by a family has been showing poor return of investment over a few consecutive years with high absenteeism of members and poor performance. The family has been traumatised by the death of the business founder (father), and dysfunctional relations amongst family members, such as lack of empathy, absence of communication and tensions in relationship.

Application of a family-centred approach

The example above can be addressed using structural and relational dynamics in a family setting. These two sets of family dynamics can help to explore the family structure and relational direction, depth and orientation.

Two diagrams (Figures 3.2 and 3.3) demonstrate the application of these dynamics. The structural and relational spaces can be expanded with more complex structures and relationships in a family.

Founder (Father/Grandfather)		
Wife	Brother	Sister
Sons	Daughters	Nephews/Nieces
Cousins	Grand son/daughter	Other relatives

Figure 3.2 Structural relationships of family members in a business context.

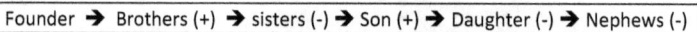

Founder ➔ Brothers (+) ➔ sisters (-) ➔ Son (+) ➔ Daughter (-) ➔ Nephews (-)

Figure 3.3 Relational dynamic in a family business indicating positive (+) and negative (−) relations between family members.

A questionnaire to identify level of knowledge and skills

A good practice prior to applying a family-centred approach is to identify the levels of knowledge and skills in this approach. The following questionnaire is designed to help a coaching practitioner to draw a plan to gain relevant knowledge, and to develop the skills to apply a family-centred approach to their coaching practices. The questionnaire is in a developmental stage and a coach needs to modify it according to their needs and expectations on achieving relevant knowledge and skills.

Q.1: Do you have professional qualifications and/training for the following disciplines? Please tick all as they apply to you.

a   Family counselling
b   Family therapy
c   Psychotherapy
d   Family science
e   Family coaching
f   Family life education
g   Family case management
h   Family practice
i   Family system
j   Any other related areas

If you have knowledge and skills in any of these areas, then write down what knowledge and skills do you have using the format below.

Knowledge	Application/skills

Q.2: When you have identified the above, then assess if they can be applied to family business coaching practices using the format below.

	Application	Yes/ No
Knowledge		
Skills		

Q.3: Draw a list of subject knowledge you may have been using in your coaching experiences and from formal training/education.

1

2

3

4

Q.4: Complete the following grids with all relevant knowledge, skills, tools and techniques needed to apply a family-centred approach to coach a family business.

Q.5: How will you align these tools and techniques with a family-centred approach?

Q.6: Note any other important skills you may need to deliver an effective family-centred business coaching.

Note:

Assessing the level of knowledge and skills

The template below is designed to assess the level of your knowledge and skills in each area prior to the application of a family-centred approach using a five-point scale. The scale points are 5 = very, 4 = moderate, 3 = a little less, 2 = little, 1 = none. Please allocate a point to reflect your knowledge and skills level in the following areas. The total of all your scores will give your overall score for a family-centred approach. You may use the template again after the application of a family-centred approach to find out any change in scores in each of these areas, and your overall score after the application of a family-centred approach.

Family life education	Family therapy	Family counselling	Family science	Family management	Family practice	Family coaching	Family dynamics

Ethical and professional issues in a family-centred approach

A family-centred approach demands careful scrutiny of the ethical framework for application to family business coaching. This is because a family is sensitive to any external intervention due to the privacy issues both for the family and business-related matters. Among other professional issues required for effective coaching are levels of competency, skills and knowledge about family science. These are yet to be included in a framework for practices (Myers-Walls, 2014). The professional issues should also include family context and overall cultural issues for the family and good understandings of family functions in a particular socio-cultural context. The task to develop a framework for the family business coaching practitioners can be achieved using a reflective experiential approach, so that practitioners can contribute to the framework using their own experiences, and reflecting on the way a family was involved in a business, and also their functional capability as a family.

A proposed framework is presented in Figure 3.4.

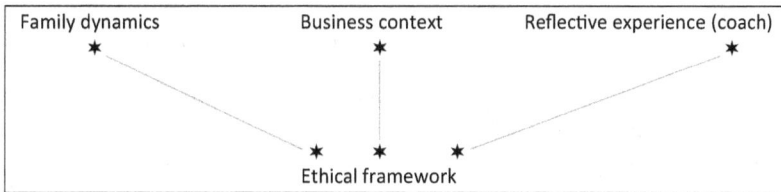

Figure 3.4 Developing an ethical framework using a family-centred approach.

A good practice is always informed by research evidence; hence, more research and evidence-based practice can facilitate the development of a professional framework for application to family business coaching practices. Coaching practitioners should take the initiative to develop this framework using their experiential learning and knowledge about good coaching practice for the family businesses.

Conclusion

Family business coaching is coined by two terms—family and business; as such, an effective coaching practice is accompanied by a family-centred approach.

A family business often demands coaching for the family irrespective of business-related issues; hence, this approach can serve the needs of a family business. A family-centred approach is characterised by an intervention for the family in a business context. Hence, the focus is on the family function as they impact on business functions. This is unique to family business coaching as the coaching approach is built around the family, and the practice is delivered for the family to improve their functions for the benefits of their business. However, knowledge about family science and skills to coach families independent of business coaching are essential requirements for an effective family business coaching practice. I have highlighted this key element in coaching practice for the family business in this chapter. My arguments are supported by relevant evidence, and I have provided a few activities for the practitioners to self-assess their present knowledge level and skills in relation to a coaching intervention using a family-centred approach. The activities can be used as a part of professional development along with other appropriate assessments for the practitioners.

A family-centred approach can unfold the complexities of a family affecting their business functions, as such, it is different to any other coaching approach, yet important to understand and appreciate the diverse approaches in coaching practices.

References

Allen, K. (2013). A framework for family life coaching. *International Coaching Psychology Review, 8*: 72–79.

Allen, K., & Huff. L. N. (2014). Family coaching: An emerging family science field. *Family Relations, 63*: 569–582.

Baker, T., & Allen, K. (2014). *Parental Perceptions of Family Coaching*. Manuscript in preparation.

Birley, S. (2001). Owner-manager attitudes to family and business issues: A 16 country study. *Entrepreneurship: Theory and practice, 26*: 63–76.

Chua, J. H., Chrisman, J. J., & Sharma, P. (1999). Defining the family business by behaviour. *Entrepreneurship: Theory and Practice, 23*: 19–39.

Myers-Walls, A. J. (2014). Comments and reflections on family coaching: An emerging family science field. *Family Relations, 63*: 583–588.

Olson, P. D., Zuiker, V. S., Danes, S. M., Stafford, K., Heck, R. K. Z., & Duncan, K. A. (2003). Impact of family and business on family business sustainability. *Journal of Business Venturing, 18*: 639–666.

Rush, D. D., Shelden, M. L., & Hanft, B. E. (2003). Coaching families and colleagues: A process for collaboration in natural settings. *Infants and Young Children, 16*: 33–47.

Shams, M. (2006). Approaches in business coaching: Exploring context-specific and cultural issues. In: M. Shams & P. Jackson (Eds.), *Development in Work and Organizational Psychology* (pp. 229–244). The Netherlands: Elsevier.

Shams, M. (2011). Key issues in family business coaching. In: M. Shams & D. Lane (Eds.), *Coaching in the Family Owned Business: A Path to Growth* (pp. 1–12). London: Routledge.

Chapter 4

Group dynamics in family business

A focused, integrated and inclusive coaching approach

Manfusa Shams and Julia Lampshire

Introduction

This chapter is designed to stimulate thoughts and discussions on the importance of understanding family group dynamics when providing coaching to
family-owned businesses. The discussion is supported by relevant research evidence, real-life case studies and a selection of activities, tools and assessments
for coaches/coaching practitioners to use in their own practice. The aim is to
help coaches to develop an integrated and inclusive approach to their family
business coaching practice.

The importance of understanding family functions in a family business
has been extensively documented (Shams, 2011). However, the complexity
of the relationships between families and their businesses is worthy of further attention in a coaching context. Whately (2011) highlights that a family
business is an organisation. The social context influences family dynamics
in a business environment. Every family business is dealing with a complex
web of interrelationships, goals and motivations. Issues can arise at the individual, family, group or business level. For this reason, we believe that some
of the ideas from family systems theory, group dynamics and therapeutic
approaches can be very useful for the family business coach.

This chapter presents critical and evidence-based discussions on the
following key questions.

Key questions

- Why is an understanding of family group dynamics important in
  family business coaching?
- What theoretical models are most relevant to enhance good family
  business coaching practice?
- How can we apply these theories and models in practice?
- What can we take from these selected theories and models to develop
  good professional practice in family business coaching?

DOI: 10.4324/9781003174721-4

Group and family dynamics in family businesses

The central feature in coaching a family business is recognition that the coach is delivering coaching to a family as a social unit, independent of business functions (Shams, 2011). Hoover and Hoover (1999) have emphasised the fundamental importance of relationship issues in a family business as they form the foundation on which the business is built. A coach with a sound understanding of the dynamics at play will therefore be best placed to deliver effective coaching, which has a sustainable impact.

Group dynamics

Group dynamics refers to the behaviours and processes occurring within and between social groups. There are a number of key theorists who contributed to the early work in the field of group dynamics. For example: Kurt Lewin (1945), who is seen as the founder of the scientific study of groups and the originator of the term group dynamics; William Schutz, (1958), who identified inclusion, control and affection as key elements in interpersonal relationships, suggesting groups work through issues at each of these levels (see Family FIRO below); and Bruce Tuckman (1965), who suggested that groups go through a series of stages in their development—forming, storming, norming, performing and mourning.

Whilst each family has its own interpersonal dynamics, it is important that the family coach develops familiarity with models of wider group dynamics. While family businesses may start out with family members only, it is rare that they stay that way as the organisation grows. For example, the business may start to employ external specialists, people on a par with the family members and who want to have their own say in how the business is run. At this point, there is the possibility of new and different interpersonal issues arising, and it is important for coaches to be cognizant of the drivers of behaviour and relationship dynamics in groups.

Family cohesion theory

An overview of recent research trends in family-owned businesses indicates that family cohesion is a strong determinant of a successful family business (Vozikin Weaver & Liguori, 2013), enhancing productivity/outputs and increasing growth. Family cohesion is defined as the degree of closeness and emotional bonding experienced by the members in the family. Olson, Russell and Sprenkle (1988) proposed four levels of cohesion: disengaged, separated, connected and enmeshed. By helping the family to understand their level of cohesion and working to identify and address the blocks/opportunities to improve this, the coach can have a significant influence on the coaching outcomes.

Family FIRO

Family FIRO theory draws on the three major theoretical constructs of inter-personal dynamics originally identified by Schutz in the 1950s: inclusion, control and integration (Haberman & Danes, 2007). They developed a way of analysing family interactions that postulates that family members' feelings of inclusion in the business and the way the business is controlled and managed can influence their integration in the business and family environments. The model has been used extensively to analyse the way families manage change and transitions. Research suggests that resilience in times of change can be increased by identifying and addressing issues around inclusion. The empirical support of the model suggests it has valid application to these issues in family businesses (Danes, Rueter, Kwon & Doherty, 2002; Stewart & Danes, 2001).

Social identity theory

Recently, social identity theory has been used to describe the psychological process in a family business context (Schimdt & Shephard, 2013). There are two main components: the cognitive component involves self-categorisation/awareness as a family member and as a family business member; the affective component relates to the emotional attachment that brings shared identity with the family business. Empirical evidence indicates the usefulness of the cognitive and affective component of social identity theory to understand "family-business meta identity" (Schimdt & Shephard, 2013).

Schimdt and Shephard (2013) have proposed an interesting notion of "family in business identity" for family members who are committed to their business and for whom identity conflict was not apparent. However, "family in business identity" is subject to a number of factors, such as length of involvement in the family business, degree of involvement (continuous and major role, or irregular and minimum involvement) and also the strength of the emotional bond with the family. Another factor of importance is the understanding of the history of the family business because this helps to generate "feelings of oneness", and a higher degree of integration between family identity and business identity.

Family systems theory

The way we learn to behave in our family of origin strongly influences the way we behave in later life. It is the first experience we have of being with and interacting with others, and our understanding and techniques for handling individuals and groups start to develop here.

Murray Bowen developed his theory of the family as a system through his research in the 1950s. He observed that each family lives by certain rules and each member of the family has a role to play, which dictates how they are expected to respond to each other within the system. In this way patterns develop as family members interrelate in certain predictable ways, the behaviour of each having a knock-on effect to that of others. Families are seeking to achieve balance in their relationships through the use of repetitious, circular and predictable communication patterns (Satir, 1983). This can be functional and effective or can become dysfunctional, leading to on-going problems; problems that could have a severe impact in a family business context.

In summary, family systems theory suggests that within the family, individual members have roles. Rules, stories and messages are used openly and/or implicitly to create and assign these roles. If problems arise, then it is not just one person but the family system that needs to change because the relationships work in an interdependent manner.

Key issues for families working together in business

The relationship issues that arise within any family can become magnified when the family is also working in business together. The coach may be asked to address relationship issues that have a range of contributing factors. These could include:

Communication	What is conveyed, how, when and to whom? Are there secrets and partial information or are all parties open to the same information?
Favouritism (real or perceived)	Is everyone treated equally and equitably or is there evidence of bias? Is historic jealousy impacting current events?
Decision-making	What is the style of decision-making and is it appropriate for the situation? Who is involved and who is left out? Who has influence? What happens in a crisis?
Rivalry and competitiveness	This issue typically arises between siblings or cousins, or when non-family members join the business as people jockey for position or recognition. There may, for example, be issues around status, role, recognition and reward.
Personality clash	Differences in character, interests, motivation, drive or behavioural style can cause conflict between individuals.
Conflict management	Family businesses may lack appropriate means to handle the conflicts that arise and hence fall back on their traditional family patterns of behaviour, for example, avoiding the issue, making someone the scapegoat or arguing.
Personal goals	Differences in life or business goals, which are not discussed openly, not shared, or not respected and result in interpersonal conflicts.

Strengths and limitations	Are individuals allowed to play to their strengths or are square pegs forced into round holes? Are strengths overplayed so they become a problem? Can people admit their weaknesses and limitations without fear of comeback? Are people given opportunities to learn and develop, change and grow?
Culture and values	What are the unwritten rules that the family live by? How are people expected to behave? Who complies and who does not? What are the stories and anecdotes that the family share and what do these say about the health or otherwise of the relationships?
Family cohesion and integration	Problems can occur when there is low cohesion and the family is quite disconnected, or conversely when there is too strong an emotional bond and interdependency.
Knowledge and understanding of family business history	As the business begins to involve different generations working together, how do they relate to what has gone before? Is there respect and understanding of previous decisions or a desire to kick against and reinvent? How do the founders react to challenges to status quo?

Whilst all of these issues may be found in different formats in a range of organisations, they are often compounded in family businesses where family history and dynamics have such an interplay with current relationships. Alongside these, the crunch points of death (requiring a need for successors), debt (requiring lay-offs and loss of money) and divorce (leading to a change in relationship dynamics) impact not only the family but also the business relationships as well.

The following case studies illustrate some of these issues in action and show how the timely intervention of a skilled family business coach can be helpful in facilitating the family to turn things around.

Case study 1: the father's dream

From the moment John's daughter was born, he said he had planned her future in the family garden centre business. The business had started small, developed from his passion for horticulture and his "green fingers": a life-long obsession he *knew* Maisie shared. He loved to tell stories of how Maisie would join him in the greenhouse at home as a child; he proudly displayed her GCSE (General certificate of secondary education) drawings of flowers on his office wall, her degree certificate in Botany framed above. All this and more was his evidence of Maisie's shared enthusiasm for the business and the foundation of his dream of adding "& Daughter" to the company brand.

Unfortunately, Maisie took pleasure in all things botanical in order to please her father. As she grew older and explored the world, she realised her passion was people rather than plants or business. After much soul searching, she plucked up the courage to approach her father and tell him that she wished to leave the business and study for the helping professions, something she had confidentially been discussing with her mother for some time. His dreams and plans for the future of the company shattered and his relationship with Maisie soured, John approached a coach for support.

With the help of the coach, John was able to recognise that he had been driving Maisie in one direction for a long time and she had not had time to identify or nurture her own interests. He came to acknowledge that, despite an extensive knowledge of plants, she did not really have a head for business and lacked any proactive drive in terms of the business, merely falling into line with whatever direction he took. The coaching helped him to identify that there was some frustration from Maisie's cousins employed in the business as they were itching to play a more active role but had hung back out of respect for family position. Working with the coach, he was able to separate out his emotional reactions around the end of his dream, from the current needs of the business, and the on-going relationship with Maisie. He was able to identify and develop a more appropriate successor from the wider family group and to rebuild his fatherly relationship with his daughter.

Case study 2: the newcomers

The Harrison family business had been built on the back of an innovative idea a decade ago. However, the unique selling point of their product was fast becoming commoditised, and technological developments were changing the industry. Whilst the business had ticked over comfortably with family members on the Board and a team of staff beneath, the family somewhat reluctantly acknowledged that they needed to inject some new thinking at a senior level if they were to survive and grow over another decade. They employed a search agency to find them a talented creative director and marketing director, both new roles for the organisation.

Whilst the first few months went smoothly as the new hires found their feet in the organisation, it was soon apparent that an "Us and Them" culture was developing amongst the executive team. The two new directors and one of the more innovative family members (AJ) frequently found themselves in opposition to the Harrison family, and consistently out voted. Relationships were becoming tense with some older family members voicing their regret at bringing in "outsiders" to help run the family firm, and the two new hires becoming increasingly frustrated at being stonewalled. It was at this point a coach was brought in by AJ as he recognised that the business could only benefit from the new blood in the longer term and these relationship issues needed to be addressed.

With the aid of the coach, the senior team came to recognise that this behaviour was typical of a newly formed team—particularly when roles and process aren't clearly defined as is often the case in family businesses. The coach helped create a distance between the business ideas and decisions to be made and the personal politics/dynamics. By focusing them on the bigger picture, common ground was soon established, agreements made about processes for future decision-making and governance, and roles and responsibilities clarified.

Case study 3: sibling rivalry

David and Henry worked in their aunt and uncle's family business, one heading up the Southern area and the other the Northern. Competitive from childhood, both took great delight when they brought in the best results, and they conveyed this sense of competition to their wider teams. This worked fine when there was a level playing field: one month David's team would be at the top, the next Henry's. However, the business invested in a failing company in the Midlands and David was given the opportunity to try to turn it around. This was a huge prize to go for, with the potential to double his turnover if handled well and an accompanying growth in kudos and status.

As soon as it was announced by their aunt and uncle, the old jealousies kicked in. Henry demanded to know why this decision had been taken without consulting him and why he hadn't been given the opportunity. As David struggled in the early months, Henry seemed to take great pleasure in his failures and David in turn spent a lot of time in close conversation with his aunt, seemingly forming an intense supportive relationship. The atmosphere between the two brothers became extremely sour, with a wider impact on their teams.

Their uncle decided to bring in a coach to work with the brothers and iron out their differences. The coach recognised that this relationship problem was part of a wider system involving all the family members. She facilitated an open discussion between all four parties, helping them to identify what was driving the current behaviour, and separating past issues from present. In time, each was able to own their part in the current tensions and recognise what needed to change: the uncle observed that he'd been driven purely by business needs and logic and had not taken account of how Henry might feel; the aunt recognised that she has stepped into a "mother" role to David as he struggled with both the business and his relationship with Henry; David acknowledged that his closeness to their aunt only served to compound the pain Henry was feeling; and Henry was able to accept that no one's actions were taken to spite him and to admit that he was feeling left out and jealous, a feeling he recognised from childhood. By separating out the past from the present, the business needs from the relationship needs, the coach was able to start the family on the path to recovering their harmony and their focus on the future of their shared business endeavours.

Case study 4: where did we go wrong?

The Walkers are a close-knit family and had set up their family property business on the basis of shared skills and experience. They developed a business plan, sorted the financing and started work. However, some years later in a booming property and rental market, and despite a realistic business model, they were not meeting financial targets.

They knew that the business model worked and they were putting in the hours and effort, so they called in a coach to help them clarify the issues. It soon became apparent that the family was too concerned about their relationships and unwilling to rock the status quo by challenging decisions or direction. This led to an over-reliance on consensus or an avoidance of making decisions at all, leading to a lack of entrepreneurial risk-taking and many lost opportunities. The coach firstly helped the family to identify the underlying cause of their current position and the impact of their current working style. They were clearly reluctant to express contrary opinions for fear of upsetting the other family members, so the coach worked with them on assertiveness and openness. He also encouraged them to separate out their workplace role and their role as a family member. Finally, he encouraged them to introduce suitable business processes for decision-making and risk analysis.

Tools and techniques: applications

Below we present a number of tools for coaches working to understand and resolve relationship issues in family businesses. The application of each tool or group of tools is explained, the model or process outlined, and examples provided to illustrate how this may look in practice. Many of the activities can also be used for self-reflection on the coach–family relationship and our understanding of the dynamics at play.

Understanding relationships—relationship mapping

The aim of this group of tools is to help the family openly explore relationships within the family and their impact on the business.

These techniques are useful during coaching for:

- clarifying differences in perception of roles and relationships
- building a shared understanding of the relationships
- identifying any underlying relationship issues and
- identifying areas of strength and solidarity within the family.

The coach can also use the technique for:

- representing and assessing understanding of the dynamics at play. (Versions i to iii as described below)

We offer four different ways of exploring the family dynamics, from the more conventional to the creative. These are:

- family genogram and business organogram
- eco-maps
- diagrammatic dynamics and
- family sculpting.

Your choice of approach will depend on your own coaching style and the family culture/business. The following questions may help you to make the selection:

- Will you feel confident and congruent using the process?
- Do you have the facilitation skills needed to manage the process and any issues arising in a way which is safe and constructive for all family members?
- Will the process sit well with the culture, approach and style of the family members/business environment?

Relationship mapping—a) family genogram and business organogram

Murray Bowen in the 1970s and McGoldrick and Gerson in 1985 developed ways of mapping family relationships and emotional/mental health states, and much information is now available on how to create family genograms (for a clear introduction, see Kets de Vries, Carlock & Florent-Treacy, 2007).

In summary, a family genogram combines both the family tree structure and the interpersonal relationships between each family member—for example, conflict, close, distant, fused, cut-off. A family genogram is an effective coaching tool to understand both the structural and relational issues in a family business (Shams & Lane, 2008, 2011). The structure refers to the hierarchical order of family members and their roles in a family business. The relational aspect refers to communication and emotional interconnectedness between family members. An illustration of this approach is provided in Figure 4.1.

Family genogram

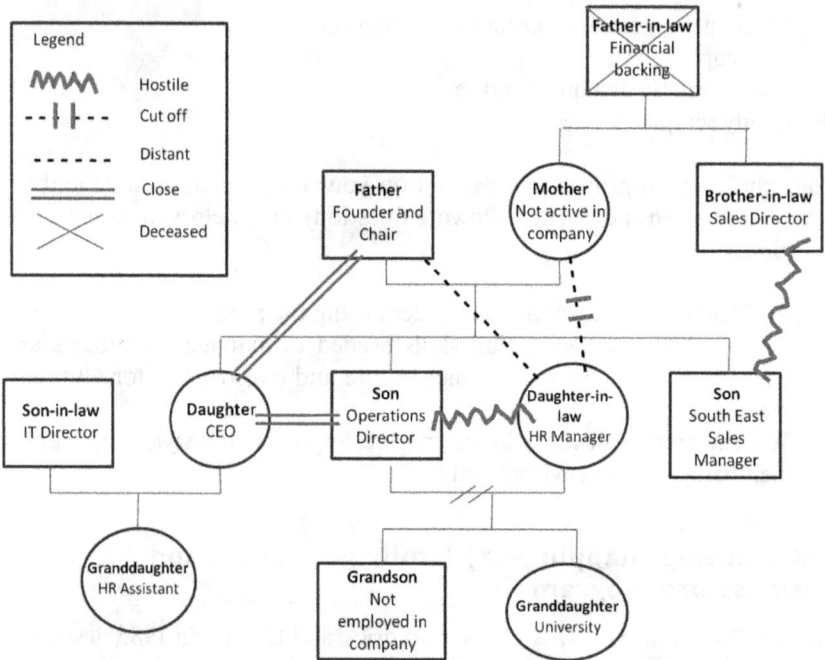

Figure 4.1 Genogram displaying family hierarchy and business relationships along with the quality of relationship between members of a family.

The coach would work with each individual to gather the information to create the genogram for discussion. Sitting alongside this, the coach would have access to the formal organisation structure showing the official hierarchy and reporting lines in the business.

An illustration of an organisation structure chart is provided in Figure 4.2.

When the two documents are compared side by side, the coach has a wealth of information to use to explore the impact of the family relationships on the business, and vice versa.

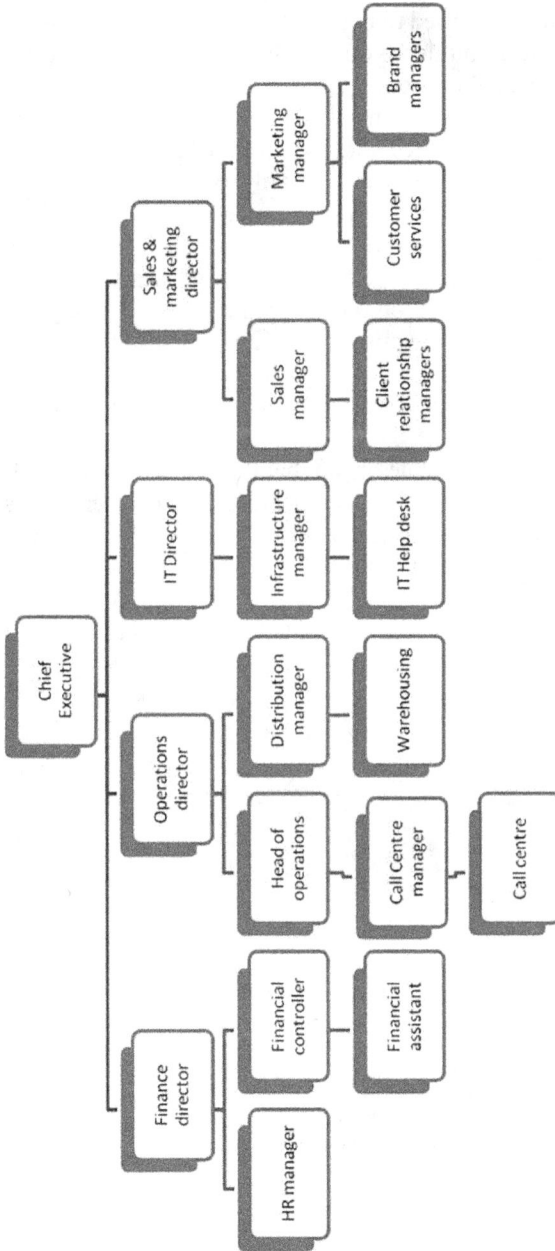

Figure 4.2 Business organogram illustrating the formal reporting lines in an organisation.

Relationship mapping—b) eco-maps

Eco-maps (or eco-grams) were developed by Ann Hartman (see Hartman, 1995). The approach is used to map all the systems that are impacting an individual and having an influence on their life. It can be useful as a simple visual aid to illustrate actual and potential issues, areas of strength/positive energy and shared/differing perceptions of these.

The coach can use this technique with individuals to look at relationship dynamics within the family and externally, or to plot the wider impacts for the family as a whole. The tool can be used one-to-one and then shared as a family group, or the eco-map can be developed as a family in a facilitated session (Shams & Lane, 2008, 2011). The coach starts by placing the individual/family in the centre of the diagram. There is then a convention for representing the different relationships, as in genograms described above.

- Thicker lines illustrate a stronger relationship; a dashed line a weaker or fragile relationship.
- Curvy, angular or red lines mean that the system is a stressful relationship.
- Arrows can be used to illustrate the direction of energy: this can be seen as who has influence and can point towards or away from the family/individual or, indeed, point both ways if there is mutual impact.

An illustration of an eco-map is provided in Figure 4.3.

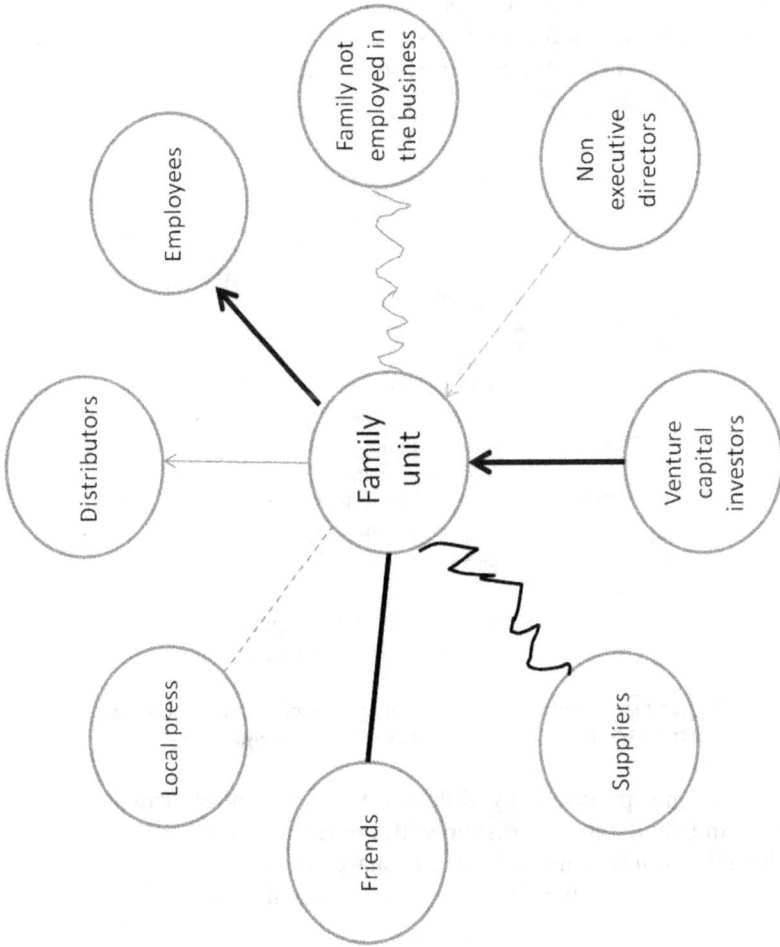

- Thicker lines illustrate stronger relationship; a dashed line a weaker or fragile relationship.
  - Curvy, angular or red lines mean that the system is a stressful relationshi.p
  - Arrows can be used to illustrate the direction of energy: this can be seen as who has influence and can point towards or away from the family/individual or, indeed, point both ways if there is mutual impact.

Figure 4.3 Eco-map showing external systems that impact a family group.

Relationship mapping—c) diagrammatic dynamics

In this approach, a series of diagrams are created to illustrate each family member's perception of the different relationships. Using a "birds-eye view" of a human head and different colours, each family member is represented. The relationships are illustrated by proximity, the directions people are facing and relative positioning (Figure 4.4).

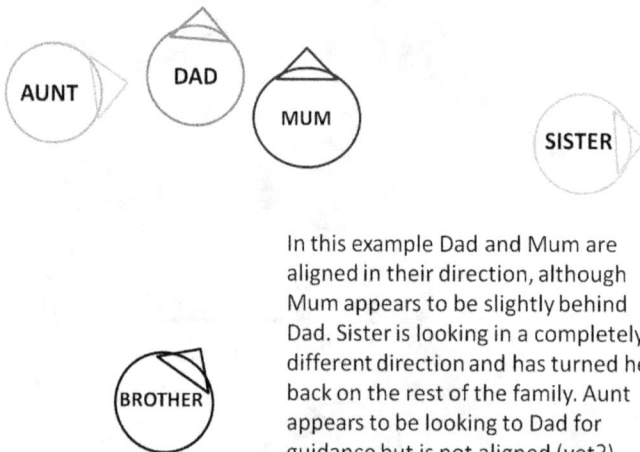

In this example Dad and Mum are aligned in their direction, although Mum appears to be slightly behind Dad. Sister is looking in a completely different direction and has turned her back on the rest of the family. Aunt appears to be looking to Dad for guidance but is not aligned (yet?). Meanwhile, Brother is looking towards Mum but seems to be quite remote.

Figure 4.4 Diagrammatic dynamics using proximity, direction and relative positioning to illustrate the nature of relationships within a family.

The diagrams produced by different family members can be brought together and shared in a workshop with the family. The coach ensures each individual is given the time and space to share their views, and the family then work together to identify/address any dysfunctional relationships.

Relationship mapping—d) family sculpting (adapted from Satir's approach to "sculpting the family of origin")

This approach requires family members to map the dynamics in the family by placing the actual family members physically in position relative to each other. This includes proximity, direction and distance (as in Diagrammatic dynamics above) but can also include body language (e.g. folded arms) and stance (e.g. kneeling) to illustrate aspects of the dynamic. Each individual in turn can "sculpt" the family group, placing themselves in the scene at the end. Once each individual has created their version, family members can comment on how they feel in their allocated position and individuals reflect on what this says about the family dynamics. The coach's role is to facilitate, collate observations and act as an impartial observer of the sculpted scenes. This approach may be best suited to creative family business environments.

Understanding personal impact—perceptual positions

This tool is a means of understanding how we are seen by others and how our behaviour impacts others' reactions to us.

This tool can be used during coaching with individual family members:

- to help family members review how they come across to others and so gain insight into how they can adapt or change to build more effective relationships.

The coach can also use this tool for self-assessment:

- to review one's own impact on the family/individuals.

Perceptual position was developed by John Grinder and Judith DeLozier in the 1980s to help people to understand the "communication loop" which occurs between people.

To explain the concepts: a "perceptual position" refers to a specific point of view or perspective. *First Position* refers to experiencing the situation through our own senses, from our own perspective. *Second Position* involves stepping into another's shoes to see, hear and feel as they would. *Third Position* refers to a dissociated position where one observes the relationship (Figure 4.5).

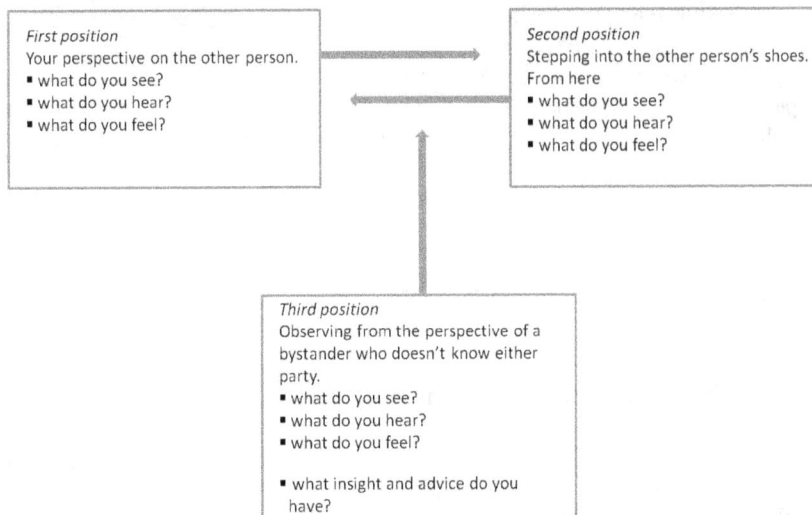

First position
Your perspective on the other person.
- what do you see?
- what do you hear?
- what do you feel?

Second position
Stepping into the other person's shoes.
From here
- what do you see?
- what do you hear?
- what do you feel?

Third position
Observing from the perspective of a bystander who doesn't know either party.
- what do you see?
- what do you hear?
- what do you feel?

- what insight and advice do you have?

Figure 4.5 Perceptual positions explaining the use of first, second and third position for understanding personal impact on others.

Steps in the process

1   An individual identifies a relationship that is not fully effective or that they wish to improve.
2   A physical space is set up in the room with three spaces (A, B, C) identified. The individual should be able to move around freely to each space.
3   The individual moves to space A and imagines that they are with the other person who is in space B and they are interacting in a typical situation. The individual describes what they are experiencing through their own senses—what they see (e.g. stance, body language, facial expressions), what they hear (e.g. tone, content, speed, volume) and what they feel (e.g. sensations in the body and emotional responses). This is the *First Position* perspective.
4   The individual now changes position and moves to space B, figuratively "stepping into the other's shoes" and looking back towards space A. From this position they describe what they see, hear and feel during a typical interaction **assuming the perspective of the other party**. They are now in the *Second Position*, experiencing how they are perceived by others.
5   The individual now moves to position C and sees the interaction between the people in space A and B in their mind's eye. Here they imagine the behaviours that are typical in the relationship and notice what they are seeing, hearing and feeling. This is the *Third Position* perspective. From here they notice anything that the person in position A could do to change and improve the interaction.
6   The individual can now move back to space A and imagine handling the interaction differently in line with the new-found insights. Now steps 3 to 5 can be repeated to mentally rehearse and refine the changes and their potential impact.

As explained, the exercise has been described using the relationship between two people; however, this tool can also be used to explore the dynamic between yourself and a group, for example, the relationship between the coach and the family.

Understanding the history—family stories

This tool is a means of approaching relationship issues in an indirect way. It can be used in coaching:

•   When it would be too threatening or confrontational to use other approaches.
•   When you notice that there seem to be a number of family stories thrown into conversation.
•   As a creative approach to open up thinking.

The coach could use it for self-development:

- By noting the stories that come up in conversation and conducting an analysis of the themes before exploring them with the family.

A lot can be learnt by hearing the stories and anecdotes family members share. The coach can work with individual family members or the family group to identify their familiar stories. These can then be explored in terms of themes and roles. For example:

- Who "owns" the story? Who tells it? From whose perspective?
- Are there any elements of the story others disagree with?
- Who has a role in the story and who is absent?
- What roles do people play in the story (lead character, antagonist, victim, fall guy, hero)? Are these repeated in different stories or are individuals allowed to assume different roles and to grow/change over time?
- How do people react to the stories? Are they positive/uplifting? Funny? Sad? Empathic? Loving? Does everyone share the same emotional reaction?
- What do the stories say about the family's beliefs and values? Are these shared by all family members?

Coaching diagnostic tool—root cause analysis

This tool is a means of identifying, clarifying and communicating the root cause of issues.

It provides the coach with a means of self-assessment:

- For structuring analysis of the situation.
- For collating information and identifying gaps in what one knows/understands.

It can also be used during coaching:

- For facilitating discussion with the family as a group.

As a coach working with a family business, it can be confusing to identify, clarify and communicate the root cause of issues. Sometimes it is necessary to help the family see when "the past is driving the present" and where they really need to focus their energies to move forward.

The coach outlines the presenting problem or asks a family member to do so. This is recorded in the top left of the below diagram. The underlying influences that impact the situation are then analysed and recorded using the following two-by-two matrix.

The presenting problem:	Family	Business
_____	What parts of this problem relate to the family? Relationships Values Beliefs Behaviours	What parts of this problem relate to the business? Structures Systems Processes Culture
Past What elements of the problem are historic issues resurfacing?		
Present What elements of the problem are to do with current issues?		

Having isolated the different causal factors, you can work with the family on a preferred future for their relationships and for the business system. This can be done by adding an extra row entitled "Future" and recording how the family would like things to be, both as a family and for the business.

Coaching diagnostic tool—business alignment

This tool is a means of identifying how aligned the individuals, family and business are with each other.

The coach may use this tool for self-assessment to:

• Record own notes and structure thinking after initial discussions with each family member.
• Identify gaps in knowledge/understanding.

It can also be used during coaching to:

• Facilitate a discussion with the family as a whole.
• Identify areas of common thinking and alignment.
• Identify areas where there is actual or potential conflict.

There are three stages to the use of this tool.

In the first stage of this activity, each individual is asked to record their own responses to a number of different questions on sheets of flip chart paper. The questions are illustrated below.

Stage 1	VALUES	VISION	PASSIONS	GROUND RULES	UNWRITTEN RULES
	What values do you live within the business?	What are you most passionate about in the business?	What are you most passionate about in the business?	What explicit expectations do you set within the business about ways of working?	What unspoken expectations do you hold about conduct in the business?

The coach then collects all the flip charts and collates the information into a table as shown below. This is a summary for the coach and forms the basis of the coach's preparation for the second stage of exploration.

Stage 2	VALUES	VISION	PASSIONS	GROUND RULES	UNWRITTEN RULES
Summary of individual perspectives	What values do you live within the business?	What is your vision for the business?	What are you most passionate about in the business?	What explicit expectations do you set within the business about ways of working?	What unspoken expectations do you hold about conduct in the business?
Family member 1					
Family member 2					
Family member 3					
Family member 4					

In the second and third stages, the coach works with the family as a whole.

The family is brought together and the flip charts from Stage 1 are posted on the wall in groups by theme (Values, Vision, etc.). The coach facilitates an exploratory discussion of similarities and differences. This second stage draws out areas of common thinking and expectations and highlights where there is actual or potential conflict. The family can see where they may be conveying mixed messages to the business by lacking alignment in their thinking.

In the third stage, the coach works with the family to identify the messages they wish to convey to the business as a whole about the values, vision, business passions and culture, and how, specifically, the family will bring these to life. Once agreed, the results can be documented for communication to other stakeholders and to use as a touchstone when making business-related decisions in the future.

Stage 3	VALUES	VISION	PASSIONS	CULTURE
Our messages to the business	The values we wish to live within the business	Our vision for the business	Our areas of passion and strength as a business	The working environment we wish to build and the way we wish to work together

Conclusion

Family business coaching requires good understanding of the intricate relationships between a family and their business. We believe an appreciation of the relevant psychological theories and models of family dynamics can help the coach to deliver effective practice. In any family there is a complex web of relationships, emotions and beliefs based on current, past and projected events and this is made more complex with the overlay of business roles and relationships. The coach who can help the family to unravel and make sense of these different strands will be doing the family and their business a great service. To this end, we believe a coach should be equipped with knowledge of the appropriate psychological models, and develop the relevant skills, tools and techniques to support this in practice. The tools we have provided in this chapter aim to ensure this by identifying practical ways to bring theory into everyday family business coaching.

We advocate a family-centred approach to coaching in family businesses, in recognition of the huge impact of the family dynamics on the success or failure of the business enterprise. The use of these techniques and theories, alongside other coaching concepts and ethical practice, should address issues in the family dynamics and help the family align their behaviours with the objectives of the business to achieve their mutually desired results.

References

Danes, S., Rueter, M. A., Kwon, H. K., & Doherty, W. (2002). Family FIRO model: An application to family business. *Family Business Review, 15*(1): 31–43.

Haberman, H., & Danes, M. S. (2007). Father–daughter and father–son family business management transfer comparison: Family FIRO model application. *Family Business Review, 10*: 163–184.

Hartman, A. (1995). Diagrammatic assessment of family relationships. Families in society. *The Journal of Contemporary Human Services, 1*:111–122.

Hoover, E. A., & Hoover, C. L. (1999). *Getting Along in Family Business: The Relationship Intelligence Handbook*. New York, NY: Routledge.

Kets de Vries, M., & Carlock, R., with Florent-Treacy, E. (2007). *Family Business on the Couch: A Psychological Perspective*. Chichester: John Wiley & Sons.

Lewin, K. (1945). The research center for group dynamics at Massachusetts Institute of Technology. *Sociometry, 8*: 126–136.

McGoldrick, M., & Gerson, R. (1985). *Genograms in Family Assessment*. New York, NY: W. W. Norton & Company.

Olson, D. H., Russell, C. S., & Sprenkle, D. H. (1988). *Circumplex Model: Systemic Assessment and Treatment of Families*. New York, NY: Haworth Press.

Satir, V. (1983). *Conjoint Family Therapy (3rd ed.)*. Palo Alto, CA: Science and Behavior Books, Inc.

Schimdt, T., & Shephard, D. (2013). Social identity theory and the family business: A contribution to understanding family business dynamics. *Small Enterprise Research, 20*: 76–86.

Schutz, W. (1958). *FIRO: A Three-Dimensional Theory of Interpersonal Behavior.* New York, NY: Rinehart.

Shams, M. (2011). Key issues in family business coaching. In: M. Shams & D. Lane (Eds.), *Coaching in the Family Owned Business: A Path to Growth* (pp. 1–11). London: Routledge.

Shams, M., & Lane, D. (2008). *Development of family business coaching skills using action models (Genogram and Ecomap) and family system dynamics framework. Skills-based session presented in the Annual European Special Group in Coaching Psychology Conference,* 17–18 December, Westminster University, London. England.

Shams, M., & Lane, D. (2011). *Organisational culture and behaviour: Understanding organisational behaviour from the structural and relational perspectives.* Learning a living workshop, Division of Occupational Psychology, 20 September, London. England.

Stewart, C. C., & Danes, S. M. (2001). The relationship between inclusion and control in resort family businesses: A developmental approach to conflict. *Journal of Family and Economic Issues, 22*: 293–320.

Tuckman, B. (1965). Developmental sequence in small groups. *Psychological Bulletin, 63*: 384–399.

Vozikin, S. G., Weaver, M. K., & Liguori, W. E. (2013). Do family cohesion and family member skill evaluation affect family business internal or external hiring decisions? *Journal of Management Policy and Practice, 14*(1): 75–89.

Whately, L. (2011). A new model for family owned business succession. *Organization Development Journal, 29*: 21–32.

Chapter 5

Generating personal and professional skills from coaching practices

Manfusa Shams and Declan Woods

Introduction

The aim of this chapter is to present critical discussions on how coaching practice can generate learning skills for practitioners to develop effective approaches, tools and techniques for coaching family businesses. The discussion will demonstrate the natural progression in learning and knowledge development across different coaching sessions. A systematic approach to understand the learning processes during these coaching sessions, from the perspective of a coaching practitioner, will be used in this chapter. The discussion will be supported by research evidence and real-life case studies. These cases show how the context in which the coaching takes place can also be a source of learning, whether a coach is able to do that "in the moment" through "reflection in action" (Argyris and Schon, 1978) or subsequently, after a coaching session has ended. The arrival and spread of coronavirus disease 2019 (COVID-19), and ensuing pandemic, has had a profound impact on the world of work and changed organisation's context in which coaching takes place with alarming speed. In turn, this has placed a premium on coaches' ability to learn "on the go" and from this context. A theoretical framework is proposed to guide the coaching practitioner to trace learning skills from coaching. The chapter will provide activities and assessments for coaching practitioners to use in their own practice, with an aim to highlight the emergence of learning skills from the coaching practices, particularly in a family business context.

Key questions

- How are learning skills embedded in coaching sessions?
- How is coaching itself an "auto-learning" technique?
- What process is involved to transform "auto-learning" into appropriate coaching techniques for family businesses?
- What are the scopes of "auto-learning" to facilitate good practice in coaching family businesses?
- How can learning progress naturally for a coach in coaching sessions?

DOI: 10.4324/9781003174721-5

Learning from coaching practices

Coaching in family businesses involves a blend of approaches (Shams, 2011), which attend to both family and business functions separately but combine into an integrated approach. For example, the use of family psychotherapy and counselling for family functions can be used in conjunction with other relevant coaching approaches, tools and techniques to address business functions.

Most coaches have an avaricious appetite for learning using new coaching techniques and skills and are regular course-goers to acquire this learning. How people, including coaching practitioners, learn and acquire new knowledge and skills is far from new, and typically follows a familiar, programmatic path, that is, participate in a learning event, gain new know-how or skills, then put them into their own practice.

A distinction must be made between formal learning and training sessions for coaches and the self-directed auto-learning arising during the coaching sessions. Wright, Trudel and Culver (2007) provide an example of the former in discussing the importance of coaching education to foster the intellectual growth of a coach in sports, whereas a review of the literature for this paper indicates the predominant influence of rich learning experiences from the actual coaching sessions themselves over other forms of education for coaches (Fleurance and Cotteaux, 1999). In an attempt to conceptualise "informal learning" during coaching, Wright and colleagues (2007) have used the term "unmediated learning situations" because of the voluntary nature of learning. In other words, the coach can choose what to learn from the coaching sessions.

We consider that skills can be gained in many different ways: formally or informally; planned or *ad hoc*; self- (coach) generated or coachee generated with the coach, learning from the coaching, *etc*. The learning arising from the interaction with the coachee confirms the powerful influence of social relationships in knowledge construction and understanding of the social context in which coaching is embedded (Cassidy, Jones & Potrac, 2004; Jones, Armour & Potrac, 2004; Light, 2004). This chapter will distinguish between formal and other learning opportunities and the different occasions when a coach might learn from them in different ways.

It is expected that gaining new skills can—and should—be a deliberate activity and one not left to chance. Furthermore, coaches also generate new skills informally and in an *ad hoc* manner while coaching. The question remains, how can coaches generate new skills in a methodical manner while also maximising opportunities to do the same opportunistically?

The case study below illustrates different learning opportunities at different stages in a coaching relationship, including post hoc learning.

Case study 1

This is the first of two related case studies based upon the coaching of Sarah (name changed to preserve anonymity).

Sarah is the CEO of a niche shoe manufacturing business, which she set up ten years ago. Sarah is responsible for all aspects of the business. There are ten employees, including an MD (her older brother), and sales and administration staff (that include her nephew—her brother's son—and a cousin). Sarah has recently hired a non-executive director to look at possible areas for expansion and asked him to help her grow the business.

Sarah has always found that she is competing in a man's world and she has experienced men actively trying to stop her from being successful in the past. She feels this might be reflective of her personality because she recognises she can come across as pushy. Men have been both positive and detrimental role models for her.

Sarah has contracted with a coach to help her step out of the day-to-day maelstrom of running a family business and help her understand how to be more successful. A psychometric personality profile completed at the start of the coaching revealed that Sarah likes to keep very busy through have lots of "plates spinning" at the same time and set herself—and the business—high targets to achieve. She recognises she can be quick to express frustration when dissatisfied and actively competes with everyone.

The coaching programme overall got off to a good start with Sarah completing, and the coach debriefing, a personality psychometric tool designed to raise Sarah's awareness of her operating style and behavioural preferences (Session 1). This tool indicated that Sarah liked to work at a fast tempo. The arrival of COVID-19 necessitated home working for Sarah and her employees and the coaching to shift from face-to-face delivery to a virtual delivery format using information technology.

By Session 2, and under pressure to deliver successful coaching outcomes quickly with a demanding client, the coach decided he might best build rapport by matching Sarah's fast-paced style. Feeling slightly daunted to be coaching a CEO, the coach skipped over the contracting phase of setting up this second coaching session and rushed to get into the "proper" coaching as he saw it. The coach challenged Sarah hard from the start of the session and continued like this for 20 minutes. He then experienced Sarah's competitiveness first-hand as she verbally attacked the coach. The coaching session came to an equally quick halt and, unsure how to recover from this setback, the session ended prematurely. The coach retreated, uncertain as to what had just happened.

Post hoc learning: Using the second stage of Kolb's learning cycle, the coach reflected on what had occurred during the coaching session. Through this, he realised that his challenge had been too early and too strong in their relationship for Sarah, that is, he had not sufficiently "established a trust-based relationship with the client". It is said that a coaching intervention should only be as strong as the relationship and he recognised that his challenge had been in excess of the fledgling relationship. Furthermore, he came to realise that he had not monitored his own state adequately during the coaching. Had he done so, through a process of self-monitoring and regulation, he may have recognised the benefit of moderating his behaviour during the session.

Learning from the case study

This case illustrates a number of points:

- Firstly, that many coaches enter enthusiastically into coaching after having completed a coach-training programme. These programmes are typically designed to equip coaches with the basic skills and competencies needed to coach effectively. This is a formal, programmatic approach to learning and can serve the coach well.
- This approach is only one way to learn; however, the case illustrates that a coach can also learn at many different times and in different ways. For example, there is no evidence of the coach to have any planning and preparation stages in advance. Using a reflective approach, the coach was able to find out that the best way to work with Sarah was to draw her personality profile. The coach appeared also not to learn during the coaching itself.
- The coach did appear to wish to learn after the coaching in this case, and this is confirmed by "readiness to learn" notion, that is, we choose to learn when we are ready to learn as well as what we wish to learn.
- The case also underlines one area that seems particularly pertinent when coaching in a family-owned business, and this relates to establishing a trust-based relationship with the coachee. While this is important in any coaching context, we believe it is especially important when coaching in a family business because of the intertwined relationship between emotionally connected people and work. Given the closeness of family relations, we suggest it is paramount for the coach to establish trust as a critical precursor to being able to coach. In this case, there was insufficient trust built for the strength of the coach's intervention.

Formal learning as a coach versus learning while coaching

Many new to coaching begin by participating in a coach training and education programme to gain, practice and hone core coaching skills, such as active listening, open questioning, extended empathy. We argue that this is necessary but insufficient for the beginners and experienced coaching practitioners, respectively.

Formal methods of education represent a small overall part of learning and that institutionalised learning is almost irrelevant compared to informal learning (Dawes, Bennett, Cunningham & Cunningham, 1996). While this view might seem a little harsh, we argue the latter is particularly pertinent for more experienced coaching practitioners whose practice may have evolved beyond basic skills and capabilities to the need for on-going learning and development of their coaching practices. The challenge for the coach seems to be what and then how to learn new skills informally?

Argyris (1991) has stated that most people don't know how to learn. If this is true for coaches, then how can they hope to develop their competency and practice beyond the application of some basic coaching models or tools? A good place to start in this context is the coaching session itself, which provides a forum and context for learning. However, a stimulus is often needed too to trigger a coach to learn. This might take the form of an internal feeling of discomfort by a coach after coaching sessions, leading to the feeling of incomplete or inadequate coaching intervention (Atkins & Murphy, 1993).

Learning through reflection and triggers for learning

Adult learning theories (e.g. Knowles, 1985) suggest that managers learn the most when they are ready to learn—that is when they recognise in themselves that their past experience is no longer proving useful in the current situation. It may take a particular event to trigger this awareness and being conscious of areas for development in their practice. This is illustrated in Case study 1 (above). Here, we saw that Sarah's reaction and the premature ending of the coaching session was the trigger for the coach to learn. This, in itself, was insufficient to show *what* the coach had to learn, however. This took another learning-related activity—the coach to reflect on what had occurred. In this case, he used Kolb's (1984) learning cycle to do this.

The coach could have reflected (with or without the learning cycle) without the critical incident with Sarah taking place. Yet this has provided a particular fulcrum for learning, as we will see with the new idea proposed in the next section.

Generating skills from coaching experiences/practices

In the absence of any evidence on how coaching practice is feeding itself to generate new knowledge and skills, the discussion will be based on the proposed "auto-learning" concept. The new concept, "auto-learning", refers to learning from the coaching practice using preselected tools, techniques and self-initiatives to capture the learning from the coaching sessions. The concept is similar to Kolb's (1984) reflective learning cycle except that the auto-learning cycle arises from the interaction between the coach and the coachee; hence, the social context of learning, albeit, a coaching session in this context is the main determinant and driving force to generate new knowledge and learning skills for coaching family businesses.

The key point here is the emergence of new learning and related skills from interactions with coachees, which, in turn, are derived from the nature of the dialogue (Armstrong, 2012), emotional display and cognitive functioning during the coaching sessions. So far, there is no known strategy used by coaches to capture learning occurring during coaching sessions. The focus in this chapter is on the coach and a theoretical framework is proposed in Figure 5.1 to demonstrate the key stages in learning during the coaching sessions from a coach's perspective.

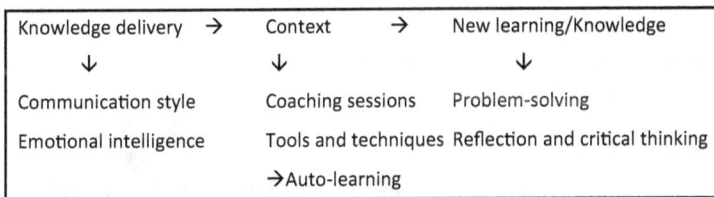

Knowledge delivery →	Context →	New learning/Knowledge
↓	↓	↓
Communication style	Coaching sessions	Problem-solving
Emotional intelligence	Tools and techniques	Reflection and critical thinking
	→Auto-learning	

Figure 5.1 Key stages in learning from a coaching session.

The idea underpinning this framework is the capacity, that is, capturing coaching experiences to develop further coaching skills both during and after the coaching sessions. The main focus is on the coach's behavioural, cognitive and emotional responses in coaching sessions, with an aim to draw attention to coaching practitioners about the benefits of learning from all aspects of coaching, and to develop skills based on their practice-related experiences. This is similar to the participation metaphor (Trudel & Gilbert, 2006), and this metaphor is gained from participation, discussions and delivering relevant ideas, thoughts, and critical appraisal of selected learning activities, and without limiting to any specific learning context. This metaphor is based on learning during coaching sessions from the perspective of a coach (Shams, 2013). We can use the metaphor to demonstrate how learning occurs and new knowledge is developed during the coaching sessions after critical appraisals of the coaching sessions, and through the delivery of feedforward feedback on the coaching outcomes to the coachee. Learning from coaching is informal learning but a powerful source for self-development and professional understanding of the coaching task (Ben-Peretz, 2002).

The discussion in this chapter has emphasised on collaborative learning to demonstrate the value of learning from the coaching sessions and skill developments inherent in the coaching sessions for the coaching practitioner (Shams, 2013). The learning from coaching experience can also be gained from informal dialogues between the coaching practitioners in a professional development context (Shams & Law, 2012). We argue that learning can also occur in the conversation between a coach and coachee during a formal coaching session.

Educational value of coaching sessions: self-directed learning

Although there is almost no evidence on learning skills being generated from coaching sessions, there is indirect evidence to suggest that coaches benefit from new learning arising from the interaction with a coachee during coaching sessions. For example, Grant (2011) has called for coaching session structure models to capture specific phases of the coaching conversations. This can facilitate our understanding of the knowledge gained in these sessions. Wang (2013) has summarised the qualities and attitudes of a coach as these may affect the way coaching practice is carried out. However, our focus in this chapter is learning skills arising from the coaching sessions; hence, it is a post-coaching learning rather than prerequisite to effective coaching as was outlined by Wang (2013).

Most examples of learning take the shape of adapting to change—where we increase our effectiveness in dealing with the environment (Howe, 1980). Neisser and colleagues (1996) discussed a person's ability to adapt effectively to the environment and to learn from experience, which seems important for the coach because the context for their learning is coaching within this organisation setting. Pedler, Burgoyne and Boydell (1998) have mentioned how a learning organisation evolves while facilitating learning although the organisation's primary role is to provide positive learning experiences for the learners. Smith (1985), similarly, highlights the importance of climate in helping adults learn. However, does the context of a family business provide this learning environment for coaches?

We argue that a coach's approach to coaching is built upon their preferred style of learning. The implicit learning need from a coaching session is apparent from the evaluation of coaching sessions, a coachee's sustained progression rate, and reflection on the coaching approach, techniques and tools used. Honey and Mumford's (1992) individual learning style preferences has become the "received wisdom" to development since. For the coach, it underlines the importance of their role as a learner and the need to be committed to exploring and developing. However, this emphasis on learning styles has led to a focus on the learner devoid from the context in which the learning takes place, and the interaction between them and the learning environment—the coaching session. Salaman and Butler (1990) mentioned that such a stance places the learner-coach in a passive learning position as it involves little effort on their part to find out for themselves the relevance, application and practical suitability of general propositions to their own situation. The discussion in the second case study below shows a coach's use

of pre- and post-coaching reflection and learning. It highlights the importance of developing a trust-based relationship to coach effectively in a family
business setting and of the value of learning through supervision.

This case study continues the story of the coach working with Sarah, the
founder/owner of the shoe manufacturing business—after the last coaching
session had ended abruptly.

Case study 2

Establishing a trust-based relationship with the client

This second case study continues the story of the coach working with Sarah,
the founder/owner of the shoe manufacturing business after the last coaching
session had ended abruptly.

Bruised by the experience, the coach retreated to safety. He thought about
the coaching and rationalised his actions. He'd contracted with the client
to work towards some outcomes and stuck to this and challenged his client
(Sarah) to move forwards to meet her goals. At first, he could identify little
that he could have done differently or better. A few days later, however, with
the immediacy of the situation abated, he was able to move into a more
reflective space and try to piece together what had occurred. In other words,
he was in a better place to learn.

He was left bruised by the experience and felt he had let himself down. He
recognised that his coaching fell short of his own expectations and, although
well intended, wasn't that useful for Sarah. He wondered if he was putting
too much pressure on himself and realised this was probably true. He was
keen to make sense of what had taken place, including from the change of
coaching context, learn from it and move forwards. In other words, the coach
was developing what McCall, Lombardo and Morrison (1988) referred to as
learning agility. Had the coach possessed more of this earlier, it might have
enabled him to continue the coaching session without it reaching an abrupt
end and damaging the coach–coachee relationship.

Pre-coaching learning

The coach looked back on his last self-assessment of competence that he'd
carried out after finishing his coach training. This was designed to help him
determine his learning needs for the year ahead. In this, his biggest area for
development was in the area of managing self. He remembered that this
competency included paying attention to the client while staying focused on
himself. He considered whether this was relevant to his coaching with Sarah
and realised it was. On reflection, he recalled Sarah's irritation at some of his
interventions, which he now realised punctuated and disrupted the session,
albeit while trying to be helpful. He had either missed or ignored these cues

at the time. He contemplated why this was and concluded that it was because he was probably thinking about the next question to ask. In doing so, he has lost engagement with Sarah.

Through further reflection, the coach also recognised that he preferred coaching in person far more than remote meetings using technology, believing that this affected not only his ability to "read the room" and spot patterns arising during the coaching, but also his coaching presence and capacity to develop a working coaching alliance effectively.

The coach explored both topics with his coaching supervisor. The coach realised that although he had contracted for coaching in person, he had not re-contracted when this changed to remote coaching. Had he done so, he might have been able to raise his concerns about his virtual coaching presence and the potential impact of this on their relationship and reached a new agreement with the coachee about how they would work together virtually.

Through supervision, the coach remembered parts of Sarah's story that had led to her setting up the shoe manufacturing business in the first place, namely a disagreement with her father who wanted her to remain in the family business in a role of his choosing. While well intentioned, the father's stance limited Sarah from realising her potential and so she left.

The supervisor identified the parallel between the coach's strong stance and the unconscious counter-transference from Sarah who was seeing the coach as if he was her father—and reacted accordingly. The coach came to see that there were signs of Sarah's frustration present during the coaching, which, had he picked up on them, would have led him to modify his choice of intervention and style. Much of this was taking place at an unconscious level, which has made auto-learning during the session almost impossible. However, through reflection and supervision, the coach drew links with the need for a trust-based relationship with Sarah. If more trust had been developed, Sarah may have felt able to raise her dissatisfaction with the coach more directly, which could have led to a productive exploration of this area and some of the current challenges Sarah was having with the men in her business.

Drawing on Kolb's learning cycle, the coach considered how he could experiment with different approaches and acting flexibly during the coaching while also maintaining presence and good working relationship with the coachee.

Learning from this case study

Learning opportunities are expected to arise from practical coaching experience. The underpinning assumption here is that the actual learning depends on the extent to which challenges from this experience are available. It would seem that people learn optimally in situations where traditional behaviour and practices no longer work. Challenges force us to try out new ways of behaving and experience the consequences of this behaviour. In other words, we learn by experience, even if we fail to learn immediately, because development based on new experience requires us to "sink or swim".

Case study 1 and 2 show the impact a changing context can have on coaches' ability to coach. Phil Sandahl of Team Coaching International sums this up well:

> Frankly, for the majority of coaches, virtual team coaching is by far a distant second choice compared to meeting with a team in-person and face to face. Unfortunately, the world of teams will not be accommodating our wishes; we need to learn to be effective in coaching virtual teams. The need for our work is too important. The mission is largely unchanged. It's the environment that is changing.
>
> (2021)

A recent CIPD survey (2020) shows there has been a major increase in homeworking over the course of the pandemic and this looks set to continue to at least some degree well into the future. This highlights the importance of context, coaches' ability to navigate changing settings and technologies, and to be able to work in, and learn from, them.

So far, we have seen that there needs to be both a context and trigger to learn but these, in themselves, are insufficient for learning to occur. McCall, Lombardo and Morrison (1988) coined the phrase "learning agility" and found that people high in learning agility:

- Seek more experiences to learn from.
- Enjoy complex problems and challenges associated with new experiences.
- Gain more from these experiences because they have an interest in making sense of them.
- Perform better because they build new skills into their existing repertoire.

Those with high learning agility are also:

- Eager to learn about self and ideas.
- Show a willingness to learn from feedback and experience and change their behaviour as a result.
- Interested in helping people think and experiment etc.

This highlights some interesting themes beyond the potential opportunities to learn within an organisation: a coach's willingness to learn; a coach's acquisition and use of feedback; and active experimentation on the part of the coach.

The earlier case studies highlighted learning at different points throughout a coaching assignment. This case study illustrates how pre- and post-session learning can be combined with auto-learning during a coaching session.

Case study 3

Post and pre-coaching learning related to auto-learning during a coaching session

The executive coach had received feedback in various forms and across a number of coaching clients that she needed to be more challenging. This feedback came in different formats, much of it indirectly, however, which made it more difficult for her to grasp. Examples of this feedback included low levels of conversion from coaching "chemistry" meetings with potential coachees and the same coaches deciding to work with her; to coachees' unexplained, disengaged behaviour during coaching sessions; to coaching programmes starting then ending midway without explanation and so on.

Having reflected on this, the coach considered that these situations might be indicative of a lack of challenge on her part. She decided to act by gathering some feedback from her coachees.

Coachees acknowledged that they welcomed this more active stance and actively provided the coach with feedback "in the moment". This provided the opportunity for auto-learning and, in this case, the feedback offered here confirmed the coach's hypothesis about the scope for being more challenging.

The coach experimented with different ways of working, including asking coachees how much, and in what way, the coach might challenge them and how they might challenge themselves, *etc*. By just using the word "challenge" more frequently and actively, the coach was perceived to be more challenging and thereby *become* more challenging from a coachee perspective. Extended and open feedback supported these changes, particularly in the coach. Feeling more confident, the coach was even more proactive in seeking feedback. At the end of every coaching session, the coach asked the coachee: "What worked well in this session?" and "What would have made it even better?" This produced variable results and mixed quality coachee feedback, however, because coachees often had little direct feedback to offer at this point in the coaching as they were typically still reflecting upon the session itself. The coach decided not to continue asking for feedback in this way.

Instead, the coach gathered comments more explicitly at the formal end of a coaching programme bringing the sponsor of coaching into the process too enabling them to provide her with further feedback.

Learning from this case study

This case illustrates a number of points:

• Triggers for learning arose from a number of different sources simultaneously: from initial "chemistry" meetings; coachee behaviour during the coaching; her own reflections after the coaching and from formal sponsor feedback. All acted as stimulus for learning.

- This case also illustrates the coach's use of experimentation—trying different behaviours and gauging their impact. Taking small steps, reviewing them, then either adopting them or discarding them depending on what seemed to be working. It also helped manage some of the risks associated with trying out new approaches, which can be a barrier to making successful changes as we see in the following section.

Generating skills from coaching practices

Drawing from discussions on the case studies for the need to identify potential skills embedded in a coaching session/practice, and the value of a learner-focused approach to gain maximum insights and understanding of good ethical practice in a family business coaching practice, we are offering a few innovative, but appropriate activities. The activities are expected to help a practitioner to place their own learning needs as one of the goals of coaching and for further personal and professional development purposes.

While a coach may realise they are ready to learn, they may be less aware that their prior experiences might affect their openness to reflecting and learning. While an ineffective coaching intervention or outcome might cause a coach to stop and reflect, they still need to be open-minded enough to evaluate the situation and take in different viewpoints and consider fresh possibilities. This may prove uncomfortable for many coaches and require courage to do so and a willingness to accept the unknown for a time, including while experimenting with different approaches as we saw in Case study 3 (above). Given this, establishing a safe environment (what Harvard's Amy Edmondson calls "Psychological safety" [1999]) seems an important contributory element to encouraging effective reflective learning.

For those coaches that accept this discomfort, there are strong arguments to the benefits of reflective practice, including:

- Increasing ownership of the material and encouraging the learner to have a more active role in the learning process.
- Personal development—through the exploration of self and personal meanings to events (e.g. Christensen, 1981).
- Improving thinking skills (Moon, 2005).
- Supporting behaviour change—offloading of the burden of unpleasant events or experiences—an "emotional dumping ground" (Moon, 1999, 2006).

Activity I

Learning levels at different stages of coaching intervention

Learning here is referring to three functional elements: increasing awareness, readiness to learn and new knowledge/learning.

Using the five-point scales below (Table 5.1(a–c), please rate your level of awareness, readiness to learn, and new knowledge/learning at pre-coaching, in-coaching and post-coaching stages. The scale ratings are 0 = none, 1 = a little, 2 = more than little, 3 = medium/midpoint, 4= high, 5 = very high.

This will help you to identify your awareness level, readiness to learn from the coaching sessions and the emergence of new learning throughout the coaching intervention stages. You may also find out your level of learning in each of these stages (pre-coaching, in-coaching and post-coaching) if you add up your score for each element under each of these stages. For example, add score from awareness level, readiness to learn and new knowledge under pre-coaching level from the table below to get your learning level at this stage of coaching (pre-coaching). Similarly, add score from each of these elements under in-coaching level to get your learning level at this stage (in-coaching) of coaching.

Table 5.1(a) Level of awareness in coaching

	Level of awareness					
	0	1	2	3	4	5
Pre-coaching						
In-coaching						
Post-coaching						

Table 5.1(b) Readiness to learn from coaching

	Readiness to learn					
	0	1	2	3	4	5
Pre-coaching						
In-coaching						
Post-coaching						

Table 5.1(c) New knowledge at three coaching intervention stages

	New knowledge/learning					
	0	1	2	3	4	5
Pre-coaching						
In-coaching						
Post-coaching						

Activity 2

Identifying "auto-learning stages"

Please identify your "auto-learning stages" during the coaching sessions according to the following key questions:

a   When did you find out that your prior experience is affecting your openness to learn from the coaching sessions?
b   When did you pause to reflect on your behaviour and may have evaluated your practice to offer a fresh approach?
c   When did you realise that you are learning something new from your interaction and communication with the coachee?
d   How did you offer ownership of coaching sessions with the coachee?
e   When did you start exploring yourself in a coaching context and the personal meaning of the coaching intervention?
f   When did you feel uncomfortable and think of doing it differently?
g   What stage in coaching did you notice the needs for your personal and professional development?

Activity 3

Reflective learning

According to Hay (2007, p. 8), "The point of reflection is to enhance capability, so time spent reflecting on how to behave in future situations allows you to identify more options and to plan for increased flexibility, with specific clients and more generally". This idea links post-coaching learning with pre-planned coaching actions and behaviour and auto-learning during a coaching session.

Many coaches find journal writing confusing and far from straightforward. This is a pity because there are many benefits from developing a reflective journal (Woods, 2011). Moon suggests those unfamiliar with this practice, "start with a journal that is relatively structured and move on to a freer format" (p. 52). Knapman and Morrison (1998) suggest items that could be used to organise coaching material recorded in a learning journal (such as a diary or notebook):

1   What I said?
2   What the coachee has said?
3   What I felt?
4   What I told myself?
5   What I did?
6   What the coachee did?
7   What seemed to be happening at this point?

8   What is the context/system in which coaching is taking place? What is the effect of this on me as coach and the coachee? How am I (coach) and coachee influencing the context?

- Record a coaching session—either using an audio recording device or by taking notes (with consent, an observer could also provide this function for the coach)
- Transcribe the material gathered from this recorded session using the questions/items above to structure the material
- Reflect on what you notice. Pay particular attention to points/questions 3–8 and your own behavioural, cognitive and emotional experience during the coaching
- Look for causal relationships between interactions and interventions; notice patterns and trends
- What learning do you take away from this? How will you use this learning to inform and improve your future coaching?

Self-assessments

The central idea in this chapter is that coaching practitioners tend to "auto-learn" during and from the actual experience of coaching family businesses. There is no known strategy used by coaching practitioners to capture this learning during a coaching session. Indeed, it could be argued that a coach's presence would be lost if s/he were to pay too much attention to this "in the moment" while coaching. Instead, we have advocated coaches make use of self-assessment activities, maybe as part of the reflection stage of the auto-learning process.

Much has been written about the skills needed to coach in a family business. Nonetheless, two areas of the self-assessment activity seem particularly pertinent and therefore worth underlining when coaching in this context because of the complexities and dynamics when coaching in a family-owned business: "Establishing a trust-based relationship with the client" and "Establishing the coaching agreement and outcomes".

While these areas are also important in *any* coaching context, they are especially important when coaching in a family business because of the intertwined relationship between emotionally connected people and work. Given the closeness of family relations, it is paramount for the coach to establish trust as a critical precursor to being able to coach.

Furthermore, establishing a "coaching agreement" is as vital for the family business coach. While it is normal (and good practice) for the client to establish coaching goals and outcomes with the coach, there are other related elements that are important too. In family businesses, there can be confusion (all round) as to who the client is (e.g. the founder, current CEO (if different from the founder) or the whole family, etc.) and therefore misunderstandings may happen as to who decides the focus of the coaching work and how the coach will work with the family. Clearly, there are many possible approaches a coach could take when working with a particular issue. It is important in this context that the coach agrees these with the client to avoid suspicion and mistrust forming. Developing a formal coaching agreement can help bring all-round clarity to, what could be, a jumbled situation. As part of this, a coach needs to understand clearly his/her role and the boundaries between stakeholders.

Table 5.2 is a worked example of a completed coaching agreement for Shalena, a newly promoted partner, in a family firm of lawyers.

Table 5.2 A worked example of a completed coaching agreement

Development goal or area for change?	Rating (0–10) at start of coaching	Desired rating (0–10) at end of coaching
1. Influence and impact: (i) colleagues and clients (existing and prospective) will think of Shalena as the "go to" lawyer on conveyancing matters as well as areas outside of this subject portfolio.	5	8
2. Time management: managing time across team, conveyancing case matters and business development activities, i.e. (i) being an operational partner leading heavyweight cases; (ii) responsible for a number of key client relationships; (iii) leading a team of 25+ lawyers; and (iv) starting to pull together the firm's conveyancing practice across the regional offices.	6	9
End of coaching programme feedback:		

Activity 4

Application of coaching agreement

Using the template coaching agreement form above, carry out the following activity:

* Choose a coachee you are currently coaching and consider the merits of completing a coaching agreement.
* Using the same coachee, complete the agreement in draft—what challenges do you foresee this would present the coachee and you (as coach)? For example, what if the sponsor's views of the need for coaching are very different from the coaches? How would you overcome these challenges?

Consider:

- What role do you need to play as a coach during the completion of the coaching agreement?
- How can you best work with your coachee? What do you need/not need from your coachee?
- What role does the sponsor play? How will you get them actively involved and engaged in the coaching while preserving confidentiality?

Tips for good coaching practice

The following tips are suggestions for coaches to improve their auto-learning ability and maximise the opportunities to learn while coaching:

1   We all learn differently. Find out how you learn best. Complete Honey and Mumford's learning styles inventory, for example, based on your knowledge about how you learn best, consider which opportunities you might be naturally drawn to and which you might unconsciously ignore or pay insufficient attention to. This will help you to maximise the opportunities from which to learn from the coaching sessions.
2   What part does the family business context play in learning? How does that impact on the coaching relationship and what can you learn from this and the family business environment?
3   Which skills do you think are particularly important when coaching in family businesses? Do you have these skills? How will you acquire them, for example, through programmatic learning or from increased awareness and active experimentation?
4   Look at your past CPD log and/or reflective journal. What activities have you learned the most? Reflect on what you notice are triggers to each of these learning points. What are the past signs and signals for you that have led to the biggest breakthroughs in your coaching?

    a   What are your behavioural, cognitive and emotional responses in a coaching session that trigger you to learn?
    b   What do you notice about *what* you learn from coaching?
    c   When are you most open to and ready to learn?

5   Increase your learning repertoire. Experiment learning at different times (e.g. pre, during and post-coaching) and in different ways (e.g. formal, informal, in the moment while coaching).

Coaching agreement form

Coaching agreement between (Coach) and (Coachee)		
Date:		
Details of coaching programme:		
What are the key challenges the family business is currently facing?		
Development goal or areas for change?	Rating (0–10) at start of coaching	Desired rating (0–10) at end of coaching
1		
2		
3		
End of coaching programme feedback:		

Conclusion

In this chapter, we have argued for the emergence of learning skills, referred to as "auto-learning" during a coaching session, and the development of relevant tools and techniques from the learning. The discussion was supported by one case study to demonstrate different stages of learning from coaching sessions. The importance of identifying the natural progression in learning from the coaching sessions to develop personal and professional skills was discussed. The chapter has also offered relevant selected activities and assessments to capture essential auto-learning from the coaching sessions. The chapter reminds us that we all learn differently and invites coaches to consider *when* they learn best, as well as how they do this. For some, this is through formal coach training and development, planned in advance. We argue that such a narrow approach risks missing numerous opportunities to learn from, and through, experience in the form of unmediated learning situations that arise from a coaching session itself. We urge coaches not to leave their learning to chance and to pay attention to their own reactions while learning. We believe these will act as vital learning cues to these learning opportunities. Perhaps the biggest question is not whether such opportunities exist, but how ready a coach is to seize them. Carpe diem.

References

Argyris, C. (1991). *Teaching Smart People How to Learn*. Harvard: Harvard Business Review.

Argyris, C., & Schön, D. A. (1996) [1978]. *Organizational learning: a theory of action perspective. Addison-Wesley OD series. 1.* Reading, MA: Addison-Wesley. ISBN 978-0201001747. OCLC 503599388.

Armstrong, H. (2012). Coaching as dialogue: Creating spaces for (mis) understandings. *International Journal of Evidence Based Coaching and Mentoring, 10*(1): 33–47.

Atkins, S., & Murphy, K. (1993). Reflection: A review of the literature. *Journal of Advanced Nursing, 18*: 1188–1192.

Ben-Peretz, M. (2002). Retired teachers reflect on learning from experience. *Teachers and Teaching: Theory and Practice, 8*: 313–323.

Cassidy, T., Jones, R., & Potrac, P. (2004). *Understanding Sports Coaching: The Social, Cultural and Pedagogical Foundations of Coaching Practice.* London: Routledge.

Christensen, R. (1981). "Dear Diary" a learning tool for adults, *Lifelong Learning in the Adult Years.* pp. 158–162. London: Routledge.

CIPD. (2020). *Embedding new ways of working post-pandemic. Employers' responses to the COVID-19 pandemic prompts renewed thinking about working practices.* Report, September 2020.

Dawes, G., Bennett, B., Cunningham, C., & Cunningham, I. (1996). *Learning and Development in Organisations.* St. Albans, UK: Strategic Developments.

Edmondson, A.C. (1999). Psychological safety and learning behavior in work teams. *Administrative Science Quarterly*, 44: 350–383.

Fleurance, P., & Cotteaux, V. (1999). Construction de l'expertise chez les entraîneurs sportifs d'ath-le'tes de haut-niveau franc ais. *Avante, 5*: 54–68.

Grant, M. A. (2011). The solution-focused inventory: A triopartite taxonomy for teaching, measuring and conceptualizing solution-focused approaches to coaching. *The Coaching Psychologist, 7*: 98–106.

Hay, J. (2007). *Reflective Practice and Supervision for Coaches (Coaching in Practice),* London: Open University Press.

Honey, P., & Mumford, A. (1992). *The Manual of Learning Styles. 3rd Ed.* Maidenhead: Honey Press.

Howe, M. (1980). *The Psychology of Human Learning.* London: Harper & Row.

Jones, R. L., Armour, K. M., & Potrac, P. (2004). *Sports Coaching Cultures: From Practice to Theory.* London: Routledge.

Knapman, J., & Morrison, T. (1998). *Making the Most of Supervision.* Hove, East Sussex: Pavilion Publishing and Media Ltd.

Knowles, M. (1985). *Androgogy in Action.* London: Jossey-Bass.

Kolb, D. A. (1984). *Experiential Learning: Experience as the Source of Learning and Development.* Englewood Cliffs, NJ: Prentice-Hall.

Light, R. (2004). Coaches' experiences of games sense: Opportunities and challenges. *Physical Education and Sport Pedagogy, 9*: 115–131.

McCall, W., Lombardo. M. M., & Morrison, A. M. (1988). *The Lessons of Experience: How Successful Executives Develop on the Job.* New York, NY: The Free Press.

Moon, J. (1999). *Learning Journals: A Handbook for Academics, Students and Professional Development (1st Edition).* London: Routledge Falmer.

Moon, J. A. (2005). *First Person,* unpublished short story. In: J. A. Moon (Ed.), *Learning Journals: A Handbook for Reflective Practice and Professional Development (2nd edition)* (p. 46). London: Routledge.

Moon, J. A. (2006). *Learning Journals—A Handbook for Reflective Practice and Professional Development (2nd edition)*. London: Routledge.

Neisser, U., Boodoo, G., Bouchard, T., Boykin, A., Brody, N., & Ceci, S. (1996). Intelligence: Knowns and unknowns. *American Psychologist, 51*: 77–101.

Pedler, M., Burgoyne, J., & Boydell, T. (1998). *The Learning Company*. London: McGraw.

Salaman, G., & Butler, J. (1990). Why managers won't learn. *Management Education and Development, 21*: 183–191.

Sandahl, P. (2021): 6 Challenges of Coaching Virtual Teams & How to Address Them, Team Coaching International, https://teamcoachinginternational.com/six-challen ges-coaching-virtual-teams/ accessed 30 April 2021.

Shams, M. (2011). Key issues in family business coaching. In: M. Shams & D. Lane (Eds.), *Coaching in the Family Owned Business* (pp. 1–12). London/New York: Routledge..

Shams, M. (2013). Communities of coaching practice: Developing a new approach. *International Coaching Psychology Review, 8*: 89–91.

Shams, M., & Law, H. (2012). Peer coaching framework: An exploratory technique. *The Coaching Psychologist, 8*(1): 46–49.

Smith, R. M. (1985). *Learning How to Learn: Applied Theory for Adults*. Milton Keynes: Open University Press.

Trudel, P., & Gilbert, W. (2006). Coaching and coach education. In: D. Kirk, D. MacDonald & S. O'Sullivan (Eds.), *The Handbook of Physical Education* (pp. 516–539). London: Sage.

Wang, Q. (2013). Structure and characteristics of effective coaching practice. *The Coaching Psychologist, 9*(1): 7–17.

Woods, D. N. (2011). Coaches use of reflective journals for learning. In: J. Passmore (Ed.), *Supervision in Coaching. Supervision, Ethics and Continuous Professional Development* (p. 282). Kogan Page.

Wright, T., Trudel, P., & Culver, D. (2007). Learning how to coach: The different learning situations reported by youth ice hockey coaches. *Physical Education and Sport Pedagogy, 12*: 127–144.

Chapter 6

Learning and developing skills from coaching outcomes

Manfusa Shams and Graham Clark

Introduction

This chapter aims to present critical discussions on knowledge enhancement and learning from coaching outcomes in the context of family business coaching using relevant research evidence, real-life case studies and examples.

The chapter highlights the key issues of coaching outcomes in a family business context. The focus is on the professional development of coaching practitioners using the insights drawn from the family business coaching outcomes and associated learning.

Using a pragmatic and learning-centred approach, the authors have used their own understanding of the benefits from the coaching outcomes from a professional development and further learning context. The need for engaging coaching psychologists/practitioners/coaches with the coaching outcomes, and the development of coaching tools and techniques using the coaching outcomes is emphasised. The link between good coaching practice and effective coaching outcomes is discussed to highlight the essential learning elements. Further thoughtful analysis is carried out to identify the challenges and risks in relation to the assessment of coaching outcomes due to data protection and confidentiality issues in coaching practice.

This chapter provides relevant activities and assessments for coaches/coaching practitioners to use in their own practice, and to appreciate the value of coaching outcomes to develop new skills, techniques and tools to tailor coaching practices for family businesses.

This chapter addresses the following key questions.

Key questions

- Why do coaching outcomes need to be researched and documented appropriately to develop coaching psychology and practice-related issues?
- What are the coaching outcomes and how they can generate personal learning and professional skills?

DOI: 10.4324/9781003174721-6

- How can the learning from the coaching outcomes enhance efficacy and good professional coaching practice?
- What are the benefits of assessing coaching outcomes in a coaching practice?
- What are the key learning issues and practice-related benefits from coaching outcomes?
- What are the most effective methods to deliver coaching outcomes from a professional development and further learning perspective?

Learning from coaching outcomes

Drawing from a few relevant research evidence in this area (e.g. Grant, Passmore, Cavanagh & Parker, 2010), the discussion in this section aims to demonstrate the need for integrating coaching outcomes from family business coaching into all other areas of coaching practice to develop coaching psychology.

A distinction must be made between the evaluation of coaching practice, usually from a coachee's perspective and/or from the service users' perspectives, and the evaluation of coaching outcomes to explore the effectiveness of the coaching approach and the tools and techniques used. While the evaluation exercise has been used quite extensively in coaching practices, however, the direct influence of coaching outcomes to develop a coach's knowledge, understanding of and insights in coaching practice is hardly documented in the literature (Wasylyshyn, 2003).

There is a fine line between the evaluation exercise and the coaching outcome measure in relation to the user perspective. Usually, the evaluation exercise is carried out using a client/coachee satisfaction questionnaire, scales, surveys, psychometric tests, etc. to obtain responses from the coachees, while the assessment of coaching outcomes is expected to be developed from a learning perspective by the coaching practitioners to improve their practices. However, there are overlapping issues. For example, evaluation exercises can provide significant insights into the effectiveness of the coaching approach, and this can be added to any coaching outcome measure to obtain a robust understanding of the effectiveness of a coaching intervention and to refine coaching practices from a learning perspective.

The self-reported satisfaction rating for coaching intervention is considered as an indicator of the effectiveness of coaching outcomes. This is a simplistic view, as it does not consider any changes in coaches' knowledge, understanding and practice-related issues from the coaching intervention. This issue is still underresearched. The growing interest in developing the understanding of coaching outcomes is expected to support further developmental work on coaching tools and techniques in the increasingly competitive business world.

There are a few published papers on the need to conduct research on the effectiveness of coaching outcomes to understand coach–coachees' relationships, coaches' efficacy and competencies, and to develop coaching practice in general (O'Broin & Palmer, 2006). Although it is a good practice to draw evidence from other disciplines about the benefits of coaching outcome measures to improve practice, we can only do this if we can establish similarity in the discipline areas, nature of interventions, tools and techniques used. The most important issue in this context is if there is any general approach to evaluate and assessing coaching outcomes irrespective of disciplinary differences. For example, coaching psychology is aiming to promote personal growth and well-being for non-clinical population groups, whereas psychotherapy is aiming to intervene for improving any problem related to an individual and may involve clinical assessments. This does not imply that there is a sharp distinction between these disciplines, rather their meeting points can be traced from the importance given to the application of transferable skills using a practice-based approach. For example, the vast evidence about the outcome measures in psychotherapy is indicating that there may be considerable value in adopting outcome measures in coaching practice (Passmore, 2008).

The key issue in this context is not so much about measuring coaching outcomes rather capturing the learning from coaching outcomes to enhance a coaching practitioner's knowledge and professional development. This issue has not yet been fully addressed in coaching psychology, particularly in a family business coaching context.

An overview of existing executive coaching outcome research by Haan and Neib (2012) indicates the lack of a systematic body of literature in coaching outcome research. This is due to the lack of any consistent approach to measure coaching outcomes as it involves diverse methods and processes, for example, survey questionnaires, 360-degree feedback, feedback reports, interviews and evaluative task sessions. However, there is hardly any research to examine how coaching outcomes are embedded in a learning paradigm, and to what extent coaching outcomes can serve as a learning tool both for the coachee and the coach (Griffiths & Campbell, 2009).

Table 6.1 summarises the key developmental issues in learning from coaching outcomes. A good coaching practice should be informed by all these essential learning elements from the coaching outcomes and a coach will benefit if all these issues are taken into consideration to design and deliver an ethically driven effective coaching intervention.

Table 6.1 Developmental learning issues in coaching outcomes

Coaching outcomes	Key learning elements	Coaching approach	In-coaching outcomes	End-coaching outcomes	Assessments
Personal	Reflective, problem-solving, solution-focused	Open-ended, learning-centred	Critical moments, deep insights, social aspects of coaching	Satisfaction, developmental needs, self-reappraisal	Self-monitoring exercise, evaluation questionnaire, personal diary.
Professional	Measured effect size, collaborative learning, developmental issues	Directive and facilitative	Critical moments, convergence of ideas, needs assessments and adjustments	Expected change, improvement, progressive, learning-focused	Selected tools, feedback, survey, peer assessment.
Family	Relationships, communications, family dynamics	Mixed-method, exploratory, interdisciplinary	Complexity resolved, insights developed, understanding deepen, increasing awareness	Change, improvement, family-focused issues identified	Feedback, survey, evaluation, pre- and post-assessments
Business	Functions, operations and development	Focused, exploratory	Problem identified, insights developed, needs assessment, adjustment	Aligned with family functions, business-focused issues identified	Feedback, survey, evaluation pre- and post-assessments
Developmental	Effectiveness of coaching intervention, appropriateness of tools and techniques.	Selected, exploratory	Needs assessment and future coaching intervention identified, personalised efforts valued, professional issues cross-examined.	Future direction and development of coaching intervention, Ethical and professional issues generated.	Feedback, survey, pre- and post-assessments, self-assessment, tools, techniques, monitored report, revisiting outcomes.

The discussions on most outcome measures are presented using case studies. However, Grant and colleagues are calling for more objective quantitative measures (Grant & Cavanagh, 2004). Can this approach be used to capture learning from the coaching outcomes for a coaching practitioner?

The discussion in this area is leading to growing evidence for the value of research on coaching outcomes. However, one important area has not yet been included, and this relates to coaching outcomes for family businesses. This is important because the effectiveness of coaching outcomes in one area of coaching may not necessarily lead to successful outcomes for another different area. For example, successful coaching outcomes for health coaching may not be applicable to a family-owned business context. We are seeking attention to explore the way the learning can be used to develop personal and professional skills, and relevant tools and techniques to reinforce learning from coaching outcomes (Shams, 2006, 2011).

Operationalising coaching outcomes

In order to trace the learning and relevant skills from coaching outcomes, we have made an attempt to define the term "coaching outcome". Our understanding is based on the functional nature of coaching outcomes and the learning elements embedded in it; as such, it is not the literal meaning of the term. Our definition of coaching outcome is the result of coaching intervention, which is measurable, observable and can be repeated using a learning-centred coaching approach.

Coaching outcomes in the context of family business can be defined in terms of improvements in a range of business metrics (financial and non-financial), which are partially or wholly attributable to the coaching. Typically, these outcomes are related to the overall goals of the coaching intervention as agreed during the contracting phase and adjusted as the coaching progresses.

Types of coaching outcomes

In the absence of any relevant published research evidence, we have reviewed a few relevant sources to identify the most prevalent types of coaching outcomes. We have found out that coaching outcomes are not necessarily the result of any particular coaching intervention; rather, we can extrapolate significant learning outcomes during a coaching session as well as after the session. Haan and Nieb (2012) have described the learning from a coaching session as "critical moments" and identified the relationship between the coachee and the coach as the single most important predictor of successful coaching outcomes. The relationship issue can mediate/offset the effects of other factors, such as difficulties in communicating, gender- and age-related issues, complexity in business functions and family dynamics for family businesses.

We would like to refer to the learning outcomes arising during a coaching session as "in-coaching learning outcomes", and learning from the outcomes at the end of the coaching intervention as "end-coaching" learning outcomes. Our classification of coaching outcomes in this context is based on the effect size of a coaching intervention both during and after the coaching sessions. The critical issue is the increasing awareness of the coach about the benefits of coaching throughout the coaching intervention stages.

Developing learning skills from coaching outcomes

The key issue we would like to highlight in this chapter is the use of learning from coaching outcomes to develop and deliver good and ethically appropriate coaching approaches, tools and techniques for family businesses. There is no development in this area in coaching psychology, and we have taken a learning approach using Kolb's learning cycle to demonstrate the significance of coaching outcomes in developing knowledge, personal and professional skills.

The proposed diagram (Figure 6.1) is similar to the framework by Griffiths and Campbell (2009) about the iterative cycle of knowledge from coaching. Our focus here is on learning from coaching outcomes, and to develop appropriate skills, techniques and tools using the learning which emerges. We are not treating any coaching outcome as a single isolated learning object—it is a part of the continuous learning from the coaching practice. We are, however, placing emphasis on specific learning issues from a coaching outcome. Figure 6.1 demonstrates how learning from coaching outcomes feeds coaching practice through a few major processes.

Critical moments (developing insights)	→ Reflection (problem solving)	→ Readiness to learn (learning from practices)

Figure 6.1 Major processes in learning from coaching outcomes.

Assessing coaching outcomes

There have been a number of approaches and strategies taken to measure coaching outcomes, for example, psychometric tests and competency measures (e.g. McDowall & Kurz, 2008; McDowall & Smewing, 2009, Haan & Duckworth, 2012). These approaches can be used pre- and post-coaching sessions to identify any changes caused by a coaching intervention. Sometimes a control group is used to measure the size and effectiveness of a coaching intervention (Green, Grant & Rynsaardt, 2007). However, there is no published evidence on assessing the impact of coaching outcomes on developing further skills or modifying coaching techniques/tools, and to map out the learning elements from the coaching outcomes for family business coaching. In this section, we are arguing for the development of measures, and the need for assessing the benefits of coaching outcomes to enhance knowledge, deepen understanding and develop insights in relation to coaching practices from a practitioner's perspective. Using the proposed approach described in Table 6.1, we are justifying the development of tools and techniques that are grounded in coaching outcomes, with examples of relevant activities at the end of this chapter.

The value of coaching outcomes

Coaching for a family business requires special attention due to the two-tier coaching system—coaching for the family and coaching for the business (Shams, 2006). The significant feature of a family business coaching is the family-focused coaching approach (Shams, 2011). We need to examine the way coaching outcomes from family business coaching can provide significant insights in emerging learning elements to develop, sharpen and modify coaching approaches, tools and techniques to meet the demands of families in a business context. An interest to generate coaching practitioners' self-assessment of learning from the coaching outcomes can meet the need for developing and delivering family-focused business coaching practice. The self-assessment can be built on both the present and previous coaching outcomes to reinforce the learning and development of insights. Although this practice is in place in terms of evaluation of coaching outcomes, however, it is still not known to what extent coaching practitioners do in fact apply the learning from the coaching outcomes to their subsequent practices, with an aim to identify and develop further skills, tools and techniques, particularly for the family business coaching.

Key learning issues from coaching outcomes

Drawing from our previous discussion and relevant evidence, we have identified a few major learning elements from the coaching outcomes below.

Effect size and success factors

There has been a growing body of literature on the effectiveness of coaching outcomes (e.g. Kombarakaran, Yang, Baker & Fernandes, 2008; McGovern et al., 2001; Thach, 2002; Wasylyshyn, Gronsky & Haas, 2006). The key issue is the effect size of coaching intervention. A high level of effect size is related to successful coaching outcomes. If the effect size is high, then we may assume that new learning may have taken place for the coach, particularly from the coaching outcomes. The question is how do we capture the learning from the coaching outcomes and to what extent a large effect size brings successful coaching outcomes, and at the same time, an effective coaching intervention?

The effect size and success factors from a large family business are presented in Case study 1.

Case study I

Coaching a leader in a family-owned business

The coach worked with F at this Middle East based family-owned business. F was appointed to this business as director of strategy, having held a variety of consulting and operational leadership roles in the past. F had a reputation for being a sharp thinker, hence his strategy role. However, he had developed a reputation for aggravating the owners of the business through bold propositions, which challenged the existing thinking of the business.

The coach was brought in to help F to understand these tendencies and manage them whilst continuing to deliver the insights and bold thinking that he had been hired to provide. During the first session, F expressed some frustration with the degree of freedom he had been given to operate, as well as the risk appetite of the business—and did not feel that much fault lay with him. With this in mind, the coach conducted structured interviews with some of the client's key stakeholders within the family. They spoke of a lack of sensitivity to some of the family context and history, which F was displaying. An example was his attempt to convince the family to close operations in certain geographies, which had historically been a core part of the business, which had caused anger and resentment amongst the family members.

Success factors

Subsequent coaching sessions focused on helping F to think about how to "win the licence to operate" and to be more sensitive to the family context and history.

Following this, and following a much more sustained influencing process, the family did countenance the possibility of selling the non-profitable assets that they had previously been unwilling to part with.

Effects size and learning from the coaching outcomes

The effect size of this intervention was significantly high to predict successful outcomes, and this was evident below from the learning associated with the coaching outcomes and intervention.

Use of structured interviews with F's key stakeholders in the family helped F to really understand a major aspect of his job, which he had previously overlooked—winning the licence to operate and influencing his key stakeholders.

Asking questions to help F to understand the stakeholders and the family history was critical. The fact that he didn't know the answers himself prompted him to do his own research and to expand his network of stakeholders in between sessions. This then helped him grow his knowledge of the business and helped him gain more influence as well.

Change and growth

Coaching outcomes in a family business context are indicators of expected change in the desired direction, and strong predictors of increases in performance on a range of measures, including personal, professional and organisation/business metrics.

The following case study demonstrates the influence of coaching outcomes on change and growth.

Case study 2

Coaching a senior leader in an investment business

X is a shareholder in a large North American family-owned business. She was recommended for coaching because of friction between her and another senior member of the family who was heading one of the businesses within the family portfolio. X was becoming increasingly frustrated at feeling sidelined and felt that the head of the business was trying to make her life so difficult that X would leave of her own accord.

The first stage was to contract with X to understand her expectations for the coaching and feedback process. She expressed some concerns that the coaching was being used as a way to ease her out gently—so the coach and X discussed what was behind this concern. During the discussion it emerged that this reflected an underlying unease about her place within the organisation and a mismatch between her expectations of herself, her "fit to role" and her perceived capability to deliver on the role requirements.

Following this, the coach worked with some senior stakeholders to get more clarity on the role—including interviews with the HR director, the senior leader and X herself. Using standard job analysis techniques, the coach put together a role profile, which encompassed the views of all stakeholders. This helped to get clarity for all parties about the expectations, accountabilities and deliverables for the role.

Subsequently, the coach conducted a structured interview with X regarding using a modification of the Critical Incidents Technique. This looked at the behavioural competencies, which X was typically displaying. X and the coach then reviewed the findings of this interview together, thinking about the requirements of the role and the impact that X was having against these requirements.

This discussion showed that X had good capability in certain aspects of the role around critical thinking and facilitating ideas from others and had a strong ethical grounding. However, she was less suited to more operational aspects of the role, which had been the source of the line manager's frustration. For the first time, during the discussion X admitted that she was aware of these shortcomings and that a lot of the tension between her and her line manager had been because she'd been unwilling to acknowledge them.

She felt a real tension between what she thought the family's expectations of her were and her own deeper needs and drives. She was most drawn towards leading at a strategic level and encouraging and supporting others, whereas she felt that her obligations to the family were to add value in a direct, operational role. Subsequently, X went to talk to the HRD as well as her line manager and during their discussions they agreed that X would take on a non-executive Chairman role of the business and one other subsidiary within the family portfolio. X initially struggled with this as she felt that she was being "kicked upstairs" and "put out to pasture". Subsequent coaching sessions focused on thinking about her underlying energy and reassessing her values and her interpretations of the organisation's own value set. She took on the non-executive Chairman role and has been enjoying real success since.

Why did we choose the Critical Incidents Technique?

The situation between X and her line manager was so emotionally charged. This was not just due to the working relationship—it reflected underlying family dynamics, which had been at play throughout their lives and which were due to on-going factional differences between different family groups. Only an objective view could have shed light on the differences between the line manager's perceptions of X as a person (based on a long fractious history) and a more objective assessment of her performance on the job.

What has made this successful?

First, engaging with X initially to address her concerns—and building trust that the coach was not being used as a stooge to effect X's exit.

Second, engaging with X's line manager during the creation of the role profile. The line manager was deeply sceptical about X's ability to deliver and about the ability of the coach to effect change. So building the relationship between the coach and line manager, and establishing the coach's credibility was critical so that the line manager would agree to be part of the eventual solution to help X.

Learning from the coaching outcomes

Where possible when dealing with issues of role clarity and accountability, a structured, agreed job description provides a common frame of reference. In the above case, all parties agreed that this was a useful document to produce, and it proved invaluable in this case.

A structured, competency-based interview can be a useful shortcut to a fuller understanding of the client's capability, their current situation, and the broader organisational and family context. Even a light-touch, structured interview can really help. Clearly, this needs to be agreed at the time of contracting.

An "interview protocol" is another useful document. This helps structure the interview to make sure that all relevant topics are covered. It also means that a coach can "bring the coachee" back to the protocol if the discussion moves off-topic.

Whilst these techniques are helpful, they are just a shortcut to a greater understanding of the coachee and their situation. This means that the coach can adopt a more effective, more "coachee-centred" approach in subsequent coaching sessions.

Personal learning and professional development from coaching outcomes

Coaching outcomes from family businesses do not only benefit a coachee. They can also help the coach to develop their personal and professional skills, and to gain significant insights into the intricate relationships between families and their businesses, including specific tools and techniques needed to meet the cognitive demands, expected behavioural outcomes and emotional intelligence of each member of the family who are actively involved in a family business. The following case study illustrates a situation in which a coach has developed insights in critical moments during "in-coaching" sessions, in this case by addressing the negative emotion of a family member.

Case study 3

B has been CEO of a large division in the Middle East for this family-owned business for five years. During this time, which coincided with the 2008–2013 financial downturn, business results have been acceptable, but market share has been lost to competitors.

B felt there were performance issues in his team and approached us to see what we would recommend. He felt that his ideas were not getting the support or traction they needed from the team. Coaching B himself was something that emerged during conversations about the best approach for the team. The coach conducted an online 180-degree diagnostic with the team to understand their perceptions of the leadership styles B was using in order to lead them, and another 180 diagnostic to understand the prevailing workplace climate. The results were not positive—they felt that B used a predominantly task-focused management style, which was leading to a climate where a lot of factors were getting in the way of their ability to perform. B did not recognise this, so the coach conducted short discussions with each of the team members to understand the story behind the data. It emerged that the team felt B had something of a split personality—at times quite approachable and affable, but also prone to losing patience, failing to listen and to angry outbursts.

The coach walked B through the feedback and he was resistant to it initially. The coach continued to pursue the line of enquiry, so that towards the end of the session, B had a strongly emotional outburst with the coach. The coach handled this by asking B if he would like to take some time to calm down, and after 15 minutes the session resumed. The coach asked B to describe what he had been feeling as B approached the point of the outburst, as well as during it. B was able to articulate a feeling of pressure and a feeling of no longer being able to hold back the urge to lose his temper with the coach in the face of the perceived criticism.

Over subsequent sessions, the coach and B worked more on this tendency towards the "amygdala hijack", using this incident as an example. They worked on a range of coping strategies, which focused on him having greater awareness of "triggers", which tended to precipitate these outbursts, as well as on managing his thoughts and how he interpreted the triggers so that he had alternative ways of interpreting situations and conversations in which he began to feel the pressure. Over time, and with practice over a period of months, B developed the ability to manage these tendencies, which led to a better climate in the team when it was measured six months later through a repetition of the 180 survey.

The coaching supported B as part of a broader programme of improving business performance within the team, and his different attitude towards them led to a change in their ownership of tasks and the successful execution of a new growth strategy.

Learning from coaching outcomes

The fact that the coach explored B's reactions "in the moment" during the "amygdala hijack" had two key benefits. First, B was able to explore his own thoughts and emotions, both immediately proceeding and during the "hijack". This led to a much greater understanding of the things, within the environment and within himself, which tended to lead to angry outbursts. Second, it led to a much stronger bond between the coach and the coachee. The coach adopted a non-judgemental, supportive stance, but equally resisted the coachee's pressure to ignore it and pretend that it hadn't happened. The coachee was subsequently more open and honest with the coach and more trusting of the coaching process.

Within a family context, these emotional responses are more likely to manifest themselves, particularly between family members. The unspoken "rules" typical of a non-family corporate environment frequently do not apply in these contexts. Emotional behaviour of this kind frequently goes unchallenged for this reason, but nevertheless has predictable deleterious effects on the climate in teams and the culture of whole organisations.

Applications of coaching outcomes to professional development

The application of coaching outcomes is discussed in this last section using an innovative and practice-based approach. We have offered a few relevant activities to extract learning from the coaching outcomes, and to develop skills, tools and techniques from the learning. This is followed by assessments of the learning from the coaching outcomes in a family business context.

Organisation awareness

Organisation awareness is the understanding of the interpersonal dynamics and cultural norms at play within one's own—or another organisation. At its most basic, organisation awareness is an understanding of the formal hierarchy and structures. Then overlaid on this is an understanding of the important decision makers, holders of resources, who are closest to the key decision makers and those who are "rising stars". There are also cultural norms at play, for example, organisational values and appraisal systems, as well as traditions set by the founders and subsequent generations. Organisation awareness also entails the way non-family members are perceived and valued by family members, including organisational politics.

How to increase organisation awareness?

As a first step a coach needs to have an appreciation that family-owned businesses are different. There are similarities with other businesses but the values and motivations of individuals and the whole organisation are likely to be different from partnerships or listed companies.

Second, a coach should acknowledge the limitations of understanding a family-owned business and must show willingness to learn and know more from the coachee, thus opening up a mutual understanding of the problems facing the family business and an agreed framework to deliver the coaching intervention.

Third, a coach may identify a trusted advisor in the organisation, for example, the head of learning and development or the HR director. They will be able to shed light on some of the unique factors of the organisation. Also, any non-family member can contribute significantly to make the coaching intervention effective, taking a third-person stance.

The following selected questions and guidance will help a coach when attempting to understand the formal structure, as well as the culture and "unwritten rules" of an organisation. As mentioned above, this can be something of a minefield, and this list will help a coach to ask the right questions.

Organisation awareness: guidance

1   What is the formal structure of the organisation? An organisation chart should be able to help you, though these are not always available. Drawing one out with your coachee or another key contact will help here.
2   Consider the informal relationships in the organisation. Depending on the context you may be able to ask these directly, or may need to be more oblique about how you find out this information, you may ask, who are the key decision makers? Both family and non-family? Who holds the resources and is closest to the key decisions makers? Who is seen as a "rising star"? To what extent are family members favoured over non-family members?
3   Consider the cultural norms at play. What does the organisation say it values? What does it actually value and reward? What is the received wisdom about what it takes to advance? What are the similarities and differences between what is rewarded and what the organisation actually needs? What impact does the family context have? How do family members typically treat non-family members? Is it deliberately very egalitarian, conspicuously "family-first" or something in between? How uniform is this across the different divisions of the business?
4   What about historical factors? What were the values of the founders? What about the influence of subsequent generations? And how are non-family members REALLY perceived by family members? What about the typical openness to non-family members' input?
5   In addition, there is an understanding of the organisational politics at play. What are the relationships like between key family members? Who is influencing whom and how? Are there different "factions" within the family?

A coach will need to do more triangulation of perspectives from different stakeholders than perhaps is necessary in other organisations.

Interview protocol

As mentioned above, it is often useful to interview both the coachee and other key stakeholders about the specific context of the business as well as expectations for the role-holder. A coach can then "triangulate" the responses from each of these interviews to form a more complete picture.

This interview protocol is the starting point for the interview—the questions are "jumping off points" for further probing and discussion. Using this, a coach should be able to have a rich and full discussion and become fully informed about the key issues, thus developing trusted relationships and building up credibility at the same time.

The following interview structure is intended as a guideline only and may vary depending on the type of family businesses, the type of coaching being considered and the family ownership structure. The objective is to have a conversation that provides a coach with enough understanding of the family business, so that they can support any coachee effectively and establish rapport and trust with the key stakeholders.

Guideline for interview protocol

Before the conversation: Review the organisation structure, company history and other publicly available information.

During the conversation: Take copious notes! Probe in enough detail to walk away with a picture of the company's formal and informal structure as well as the demands and challenges, which a coachee is likely to be facing.

Summarise the top three to four themes you think you have picked up to ensure understanding and finish with "is there anything else I should know?"

After the conversation: Review your notes and your summary. Write up the overall "themes", formal, informal structures and cultural and historical factors.

Interview protocol

Strategy questions

- First, what is the strategy of the company as you see it?
- Are there viable alternative scenarios being considered?
- How have recent economic/marketplace events affected the company?

Culture and organisational awareness questions

- How would you describe the company's current culture?
- How universal do you see this as being?
- What current and historical factors do you think have impacted on the culture?
- What attributes do you feel the organisation values in its employees? What is encouraged? What is actively discouraged?

Individual's situation questions

- Do you feel that all the key stakeholders for [coachee's name] see the strategy the same way? If not, what are the key differences?
- What challenges do you anticipate [coachee's name] will face when executing the strategy?

- What are the key behaviours/traits that will be necessary for [coachee's name] to execute the strategy? (Look for five or six. Probe for actual, measurable behaviours rather than vague value statements).
- Probe further for any information around strategy contribution, challenges, opportunities, etc. that may flow from the conversation.

Visual guide/map

In family business coaching, a coach can benefit from the use of a visual guide/map to trace changes in their coaching approach and practice, as well as developing new knowledge and insights during the process of the coaching intervention.

The visual guide (Table 6.2) can direct the pathway to capture relevant learning and understanding of coaching-related issues. This can also serve as a need assessment tool for a coach to undertake personal and professional development. The validity of such a guide and the effectiveness of the application to make changes/improvement remains to be established through research- and practice-based evidence. However, evidence will be accumulated only when any such effort is endorsed by the coaching practitioners. Therefore, our effort here is to generate interest by developing a guide so the guide's utility and appropriateness can be explored, and a collective initiative can be taken to apply the visual guide to coaching family businesses.

We have provided an example below. A coach will find this guide useful to check the extent of knowledge and understanding, skills and experiences they may have in relation to their coaching practice and can draw a map of missing areas in the visual guide to include in their professional development.

Table 6.2 A visual guide for effective coaching intervention

In-coaching	Approaches	Learning	Family dynamic
Critical moments	Alignment	Ethical scrutiny	Communication style
Needs development	Blended	Professional standard	Values and traditions
Personal awareness	Interpersonal	Professional skills	Cohesion
Professional boundary	Interdisciplinary	Personal development	Integration
	Multidisciplinary	New Knowledge	Leadership
	Family-focused	Reflective	Role behaviour
	Integrated	Experiential	

Graphical illustration of coaching outcomes

A useful tool to assess both the effect size and success factors of coaching outcome is a graphical illustration of coaching outcomes against selected parameters (see Figure 6.2). The example below can be used on a graph on which coaching outcomes are represented on the *x*-axis; and effect size, success factors, change, growth and alignment are on the *y*-axis. As such, it will be possible to trace the interaction between each of these key areas on coaching outcomes; for example, if the effect size is high on a graph, then the change and growth may also increase, but alignment (family and business) may remain static.

An example of this graph is presented in Figure 6.2.

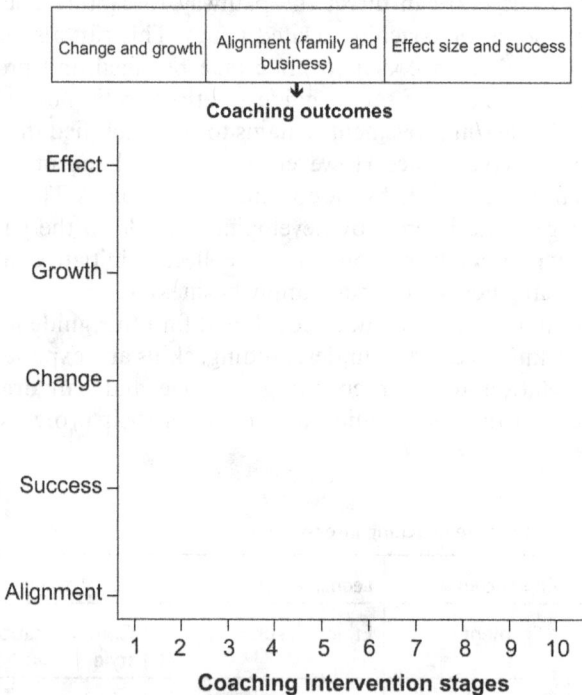

Figure 6.2 Graphical illustration of coaching outcomes against selected factors.

Assessing learning from coaching outcomes—developmental template

The benefits of using coaching outcomes to map out key learning elements and developmental issues are drawn using a template overleaf. The aim is to demonstrate the process of identifying and selecting major areas in learning, and to propose a new knowledge gathering exercise from coaching outcomes.

A template can facilitate the process of learning from a coaching outcome because the coach will have predetermined descriptors of learning to check against their progress in learning from the coaching outcomes. The template is a "progressive" document for a coach to add and amend when it is used, so as to assess the learning and developmental issues from the coaching outcomes.

To use the template, a coach can assess to what extent coaching outcomes may have provided new knowledge, reflection, critical thinking, etc. under "learning area". Following this, a coach can do the same for personal development—to what extent coaching outcomes may have enhanced efficacy, motivation … of the coach, and so on. The coach can use either a tick or a rating method here. The template is a useful way to assess and summarise positive learning benefits from coaching outcomes.

The template contains seven major areas in coaching outcomes: learning, personal development, professional development, impact, practice, advancement ethics and professional standards. The selected sub-areas under each of these major areas represent the specific learning from the coaching outcomes. Using a self-assessment approach, a coach can explore to what extent they have achieved these areas from a coaching outcome, for example, if new knowledge under learning area (1) is generated then efficacy under personal development area (2) may improve, and this can lead to identifying coaching practitioners' needs assessment under professional development (3). A coach can use each sub-area as a stand-alone learning/professional skill for each major area in this template. For example, to what extent the learning from the coaching outcomes has helped to maintain ethical and professional standards (7), and how the learning from the coaching outcome has an impact (4) on growth in practice and increased awareness of the benefits of learning, and so on.

Table 6.3 Developmental template for assessing learning from the coaching outcomes

1. Learning	2. Personal development	3. Professional development	4. Impact	5. Practice	6. Advancement	7. Ethics and professional standards
New knowledge	Efficacy	Needs assessment	Growth	Evidence-building	Coaching approach	Application
Reflection	Motivation	Skills update	Increasing awareness	Management organisation	Coaching techniques and tools	Maintenance
Critical	Commitment	Confidentiality Data protection	Knowledge enhance-ment	Record keeping	Interaction and communication	Enhancement
Analytical	Insights	Alignment (family to business)	New skills	Ethical scrutiny	Emotional intelligence	Inclusion and integration

Tips for good coaching practice within family businesses

We are proposing a few important and relevant tips for coaching within family businesses below. The tips are drawn from the second author's extensive coaching experience with family businesses. The aim is to highlight the effective delivery of family business coaching so that this can lead to an effective coaching outcome. An effective outcome will then serve as an appropriate learning tool for the coaching practitioners.

Tips

- Remember the unique family context for this company—not all family-owned businesses are the same but there are some common characteristics too.
- Don't make assumptions about the context and don't be afraid to ask for clarification.
- Be even more scrupulous about confidentiality than you would normally be.
- Remember that coachees may take longer to trust the coach than in other businesses.
- Always be sensitive to your coachees' needs as they are involved in an emotionally driven family business.
- Be aware of your professional boundaries and ethical standards so that privacy is not invaded and mutual respect is established—without deviating from high professional standards in the delivery of the coaching intervention.
- Keep the option open to debrief and provide appropriate feedback on coaching.
- Learn from the outcomes and increase your readiness to learn as the coaching progresses.
- Develop personal tools to capture in-coaching and end-coaching learning outcomes.
- Share your thoughts, understanding and knowledge with your colleagues and promote collaborative learning in developing coaching practice for family businesses.

Conclusion

In this chapter, we have argued for the learning benefits from coaching outcomes in the context of family businesses. It is important to identify learning and knowledge gained from both "in-coaching" and "end-coaching" sessions to develop personal and professional skills and practice-related understanding. The discussion has highlighted the importance of understanding effect size and success factors of coaching outcomes, as well as change and growth in practices after the successful coaching intervention. The subject of coaching outcomes is an important learning area in coaching psychology and more research should be focused on this area. It is important to develop practice-related professional activities and assessments from coaching outcomes to enhance and promote good and ethical practice in family business coaching. A coaching outcome is not an end product but a stage of continuous learning in coaching. The immense value of coaching outcomes to improve knowledge, understanding and practice has been emphasised.

References

Grant, A., & Cavanagh, M. J. (2004). Toward a profession of coaching; sixty five years of progress and challenges for the future. *International Journal of Evidence Based Coaching and Mentoring, 2*(1): 1–16.

Grant, A. M., Passmore, J., Cavanagh, M., & Parker, H. (2010). The state of play in coaching today; a comprehensive review of the field. *International Review of Industrial and Organizational Psychology, 25*: 125–167.

Green, L. S., Grant, A. M., & Rynsaardt, J. (2007). Evidence-based coaching for senior high school students. *International Coaching Psychology Review, 2*(1): 24–32.

Griffith, K., & Campbell, M. (2009). Discovering, applying and integrating: The process of learning in coaching. *International Journal of Evidence Based Coaching and Mentoring, 7*: 16–30.

Haan, D. E., & Neib, C. (2012). Critical moments in a coaching case study: Illustrations of a process research model. *Consulting Psychology Journal: Practice and Research, 64*: 198–224.

Haan, D. E., & Duckworth, A. (2012). Signalling a new trend in executive coaching outcome research. *International Coaching Psychology Review, 8*(1): 6–19.

Kombarakaran, F. A., Yang, J. A., Baker, M. N., & Fernandes, P. B. (2008). Executive coaching: It works! *Consulting Psychology Journal: Practice and Research, 60*: 78–90.

McDowall, A., & Kurz, R. (2008). Effective integration of 360 degree feedback into the coaching process. *The Coaching Psychologist, 4*(1): 7–19.

McDowall, A., & Smewing, C. (2009). What assessments do coaches use in their practice and why? *The Coaching Psychologist, 5*: 98–103.

McGovern, J., Lindemann, M., Vergara, M., Murphy, S., Barker, L., & Warrenfeltz, R. (2001). Maximizing the impact of executive coaching: Behavioural change, organizational outcomes, and return on investment. *The Manchester Review, 6*: 1–9.

O'Broin, A., & Palmer, S. (2006). The coach-client relationship and contributions made by the coach in improving coaching outcome. *The Coaching Psychologist, 2*: 16–21.

Passmore, J. (2008). *The Character of Workplace Coaching: The Implications for Coaching Training and Practice.* Stratford: University of East London.

Shams, M. (2006). Approaches in business coaching: Exploring context-specific and cultural issues. In: M. Shams & P. Jackson (Eds.), *Developments in Work and Organizational Psychology* (pp. 228–244). The Netherlands: Elsevier.

Shams, M. (2011). Key issues in family business coaching. In: M. Shams & D. Lane (Eds.), *Coaching in the Family Owned Business: A Path to Growth* (pp. 1–12). London: Karnac.

Thach, E. C. (2002). The impact of executive coaching and 360 feedback on leadership effectiveness. *Leadership & Organization Development Journal, 23*: 205–214.

Wasylyshyn, M. K. (2003). Executive coaching: An outcome study. *Consulting Psychology Journal: Practice and Research, 55*: 94–106.

Wasylyshyn, M. K., Gronsky, B., & Haas, W. (2006). Tigers, stripes, and behavior change: Survey results of a commissioned coaching program. *Consulting Psychology Journal: Practice and Research, 58*: 65–81.

Chapter 7

Interdisciplinary approaches and transferable skills in family business coaching

Manfusa Shams and Judit Varkonyi-Sepp

Introduction

The aim of this chapter is to present critical discussions on how family business coaching practice can be benefitted from the application of interdisciplinary approaches. The discussion highlights the benefits of transferable interdisciplinary skills in coaching family businesses and the value of interdisciplinary contributions to develop tools, techniques and skills for family business coaching. The term "interdisciplinary" here implies the use of original concepts, techniques and theories from different disciplines to plan, develop and apply coaching approaches, tools and techniques for family business coaching, with an appropriate attention to maintain the originality of the interdisciplinary contributions. In essence, we are looking at the original material through the lens of another discipline. Examples of interdisciplinary contributions are the application of counselling and psychotherapy techniques to coaching practices or the use of knowledge and techniques from economics in the family business coaching practice.

The focus in this chapter is to identify how interdisciplinary contributions to coaching are leading to the development of transferable skills. The critical questions are, what techniques are used to generate and identify transferable skills? And, how are these skills providing improved coaching interventions for family businesses? For example, some skills used in family therapy can be transferred to family business coaching as it involves a family (Allen, 2013). Similarly, counselling skills are embedded in coaching, and psychotherapeutic techniques are in frequent use in coaching. A coach with knowledge about economic principles can facilitate the development of a guide to sustainable family business. These examples are evidence that interdisciplinary techniques might be the best source to develop transferable coaching skills.

Transferable skills can be generic and subject-specific, formative (developmental skills), summative (end product of the developmental skills), additive (additional skills to existing ones), integrated (inclusion of all relevant interdisciplinary skills in a coaching intervention), multi-dimensional/focused (diverse skills with a common focus). In this chapter, we are addressing how

DOI: 10.4324/9781003174721-7

an integrated interdisciplinary approach can help us identify the important contributions from different related disciplines to develop and advance good practice in family business coaching.

The critical discussion is supported by real-life case studies and examples from selected related disciplines. The chapter is providing relevant activities and assessments for coaching practitioners to use in their own practices.

Key questions

- How are skills generated using interdisciplinary approaches in coaching practices?
- How can the skills from another related discipline be transferred to develop coaching tools and techniques for family businesses?
- What are the benefits of applying an integrated interdisciplinary approach in family business coaching?
- What interdisciplinary subject areas are demonstrating significant influences on delivering successful coaching interventions for the family businesses?
- Why are interdisciplinary skills useful and important to deliver ethical and effective family business coaching?

Interdisciplinary contributions

Coaching can be used in any discipline; as such, it has a multipurpose focus. For example, sports coaching has been in use for a prolonged period. There are major developments in theorising sports coaching and mentoring, and this has been dominating the field of higher education as a part of professional development programme (Grant, 2006; Parker, Hall & Kram, 2008). This is used as a pillar of talent management in many other organisations. Individual coaching services are also growing in demand. The increasing use of coaching in diverse subject areas and organisations is supposed to provide a fertile ground on which discipline-focused coaching tools and techniques can be developed.

Despite the diversity in coaching approaches, there are a few fundamental issues shared by all disciplines and organisations in their practices. These are levels of engagement, who is coaching and how, and the types of coaching—skills, performance, development or life coaching (Segers, Vloeberghs & Henderickx, 2011). We can explore the benefits of using an interdisciplinary technique in coaching. For example, coaching using an economic perspective gives emphasis on demands and supply aspects; as such, coaching is delivered on the basis of what is on demand and the capacity to meet the demand from the supplier/human resources/coach. The importance of an indigenous approach in coaching culturally diverse groups has been evident in the first author's research with British Asian family businesses in England

(Shams, 2006). The research has provided significant insights into the use of cultural-specific approaches, values and tools by a family business. The need for delivering interdisciplinary coaching approaches using culturally specific tools and techniques to facilitate the coaching process was evident in this research. Another example can be drawn from the contribution of family life education discipline (Allen, 2013) to provide effective coaching as it involves the application of family life knowledge to a family in a business context.

A coaching practice should be flexible enough to accommodate any alternative approaches and strategies to deliver an effective coaching intervention. A coach is continuously negotiating with the coachee and the coaching environment to offer the best practice; hence, it is often necessary to replace the original approaches and techniques to serve the needs of the coachee, and to meet the changing environment. This is part of the good coaching practice and an important area of learning for the coaching practitioners.

Coaching psychology is developing fast using interdisciplinary knowledge and techniques. It is becoming increasingly difficult to pinpoint contributions from a single discipline due to the merge of disciplines to offer an integrated and effective coaching intervention for improving family businesses around the world. However, it is possible to identify the discipline-focused approaches, tools and techniques in family business coaching using the dominant contributions from a diverse set of disciplines (e.g. psychology, psychotherapy, economics, business studies, etc.). We have selected a few major interdisciplinary contributions to family business coaching practice, and the discussion is indicating their unique place in developing good practice in family business coaching.

Family therapy and counselling

Family therapy and counselling works with people in intimate relationships to help change and development. The simplest way to describe the difference between therapy and counselling is that therapy might be a longer and sometimes deeper process. The relevant theories are focusing on individuals (e.g. psychodynamic approach), interactions between individuals (e.g. experiential approach) or the family systems as a whole (e.g. Milan school), as a source of the problem (Goldenberg & Goldenberg, 2004). In family business coaching, it is useful to consider the family as a psychosocial system as this makes it easier to look for similarities and differences between the family and a business organisation. Identifying and discussing these differences with the clients can help them reflect on what characteristics, for example, roles, skills, experiences, identities, attitudes, communication channels and so on are transferable from the family context to the business, and this may aid achieving the coaching objectives. At the end of this chapter, a simple activity is presented to detect these similarities and differences and to facilitate thinking about the impact of transferring the elements.

Transactional analysis

Eric Berne's (1964) theory focuses on "transactions" between individuals as the smallest units of interactions that can be observed and studied. According to Berne, each individual has three ego states, Parent, Adult and Child, which are largely shaped through childhood experiences. Adult–Adult transactions are rational and objective, mostly information-focused. In the Parent–Child transactions, one is dependent and the other is nurturing. Most interactions however are much more complex and might involve many different ego states even in one set of interactions, leading to "crossed transactions". Berne also emphasised the importance of non-verbal communication and social action, that is, one person recognising the other verbally or non-verbally, referred to as "stroke". Stroke satisfies a fundamental human need of social recognition and even a negative stroke, such as a frown or an insulting word can be better than no stroke at all.

The transactional analysis model is particularly useful in the family business-coaching context because there are pre-existing relationships between members in a non-business context (i.e. the family) and there might be automated "reflexes" in their interactions. For example, when one person makes a mistake, the other's automatic reaction can be: "you are so stupid, you can't do anything yourself!"—this is a Parent–Child transaction. Instead of this, clients can be invited to think of an Adult–Adult transaction, for example, "I see you made this mistake. Is there anything that can be learned from this situation so that it does not happen next time?" The concept of stroke can bring positive impact on family members relationship, for example, if family members do not have the habit of praising each other, then they can learn to make a conscious effort to acknowledge each other's contributions to their family business.

Group counselling

The learning from group counselling is very useful when working with family members. The coach must keep a watchful eye and sharp ear on what is going on under the surface and has to artfully manage bringing these processes to the exterior. Such processes can be hidden agendas of members or cliques in the group. It is likely to be felt as an unexplained, growing tension or getting stuck in the work process. Usually, the tension grows to the level of explosion, sometimes leading to confrontations and heightened emotions. A coach can deal with the unexpected emotional explosion using group counselling techniques to make it a positive experience and enhanced learning. Conflicts between group members or sub-groups are best addressed early. It is also important to talk openly about the conflict, associated emotions and thoughts. Sometimes group members prefer to focus, comment, hypothesise about or criticise other members. In most contexts, however, working in groups is most efficient if members focus on their own feelings and thoughts, learn to express these effectively and listen openly to other members. Such group dynamics can often be detected in families, so these experiences in group counselling are easily transferable to family business coaching. Similarly, to group counselling, it may be useful to create some rules, such as limiting discussion to business-related issues and family dynamics affecting business function only.

Organisational culture

Organisational culture is the behaviour of people within an organisation and the beliefs that people attach to these behaviours. Organisations can be characterized by how they provide a supportive culture and how strongly their members feel they belong to the organisation.

One of the most popular theories is Schein's (1992) description of the cognitive levels of the organisational culture, describing features that are easily detectable to the observer (e.g. dress code, office layout and so on), a more covert level (e.g. values that can be understood through stories, rituals, myths) and "unspoken rules" that are really hard to detect but which might reinforce paradoxical behaviour in the organisation. It might be, for example, that the family business on the surface operates a democratic leadership but an underlying culture is not to challenge senior members so there is no real counterbalance to their decisions or actions. Another theory is Handy's (1976) categorisation linking organisational structure with organisational culture. The categories are: power structure when the power is with a few selected individuals where there is a small number of rules and decisions are made fast; role culture where authority is linked with roles, there are robust rules and procedures and the structure and operations are consistent and clear; task culture where expert teams are formed to execute well-defined tasks; and person culture which is built on individualism and personal excellence. There is an optimal environment for each of these cultures and depending on the type of the family business, one or the other might be more beneficial. For example, a family art business could perform ideally in the person culture whilst a grocery business might be more operational with role culture.

Emotional intelligence

Emotional intelligence can be described as one's ability to monitor their own and other people's emotions, differentiate between different emotions and label them correctly and to use these observations to guide their thinking and behaviour. Salovey and Maher (1990) identified the factors of emotional intelligence as the perception of emotion, the ability to reason using emotions, the ability to understand emotions and the ability to manage emotions. Emotional intelligence helps us to become self-aware and socially aware, and manage our relationships and ourselves. It also affects our physical and mental health, our performance at work and our relationships. Emotional intelligence in a family business can help more efficient communication, reduce stress and create more productive teams. Emotional intelligence of both individuals and teams can be increased, for example, in family business coaching sessions, discussion of reactions to different views and expressed emotional responses of different members can help to raise the members' emotional intelligence.

Business management

Benjamin Franklin famously said, "If you fail to plan, you are planning to fail!" Managing a family business is a demanding task for family members. Family businesses often emerged from a vision or force of circumstances without professional business evaluation, for example, a viable business plan. It is likely that a family is asking for a coach's help because they cannot work out a solution to their progress or find any alternatives to crack a problem.

Metaphors are often used in coaching and can be utilised to help business thinking and planning. For example, a memory the family cherish was a time when they were truly together during a round trip through Europe. We can invite this family, for example, to think about their business as if they were going on a trip again.

What would they need to do to prepare for and successfully complete the trip?

- Define the destination.
- Have a map of how they get there.
- Plan the journey, preferably step by step.
- Calculate the expected costs.
- Identify where they will finance the journey from.
- Discuss who will have what role and function in the planning and during the journey.
- Identify who would be the leader. Is everyone in agreement?
- Agree on the rules.

Robust planning is a vital element of successful management but it is also important how the organisation (in this case the family business team) functions. Planning for the trip reveals how this team is working together. A coach can observe, reflect and discuss with the family how they work as a team, for example:

- Are they appraising each other, do they recognise knowledge, skills, talents, contributions? Are these transferable to the family business?
- Do family members recognise each other's needs?
- Do family members express their needs?

- How is failing addressed? What is the impact of failure on the family as a team?
- What else characterises their communication?

At each stage of this work there is learning for the family business, both to link the business skills identified in the metaphorical journey with the family business and to separate roles and behaviours that are part of family functioning and those that characterise effective business partnership. It is important to discuss, get family members to reflect and take the learning after each session.

Family business coaching: an integrated interdisciplinary approach

This section aims to demonstrate how a blend of selected interdisciplinary contributions can provide an integrated approach to coach family businesses, in which coaching a family as well as their business is addressed separately to highlight their interdependencies (Shams, 2011). A case study is presented below to highlight the use of interdisciplinary techniques in family business coaching. The techniques referred to in the case study are explained in detail later in this chapter.

Case study 1: family culture vs. organisational culture

A case study in family business coaching is given in Appendix 7.1. A brief description of the stages of the coaching process and the techniques used in this case is given below.

Summary of case study 1

Family business: Eve and Steve

Eve and Steve set up a business in responding to economic pressures. They did not have business experience and they did not think they had business skills at all. Despite a steady clientele, their business was losing money and they had to tap into their life savings. Eve and Steve sought coaching to help them turn the business into a sustainable enterprise. In-depth analysis pointed to the need to find transferable business skills and to review how family structure affects the business context. Although Eve and Steve had their children as business partners, they preserved the family structure in their business. This prevented family members from building business-focused partnerships and from redistributing responsibilities utilising individual strengths. Coaching helped family members identify their values, discover their skills transferable from private experiences to business and rebuild the business structure to ensure sustainability. The outcome of coaching was the establishment of a sustainable business through recognition and conscious application of transferable skills and redistribution of business responsibilities amongst family members. Results of the coaching work perpetuated strongly at the one-year follow-up interview.

Coaching intervention: The following stages were followed to address the problem in the management and operation of the family business.

Stage 1: exploration and contracting

- Exploring the client's objectives: what do they expect from coaching.
- Exploring and agreeing on what to contract for: what is the source of the problem.
- Agreeing on who to contract with: who else is part of the problem the business is seeking coaching for, do they need to be part of the coaching process.

Techniques used: one-to-one interviews, a group session to agree objectives.

Stage 2: the coaching process

- Identifying the current state and the desired state.
- Identifying core values and how these are maintained in the current state.
- Identifying internal and external resources: creating an inventory of skills and knowledge both on personal and business level, identifying transferability, analysing opportunities, threats, strengths and weaknesses.
- Reflecting: re-enforcing discoveries and learning, how these relate to current problem.
- Planning the road from current state to desired state.
- Taking action.

Techniques used: transactional analysis, increasing positive emotions, comparison of family and business characteristics, value elicitation, SWOT analysis, skills inventory, and identification of transferable skills.

Stage 3: follow-up evaluation

- Evaluating progress: follow-up on progress at a predefined time-point after coaching work completed (six months to one year).

Techniques used: group interview with family members involved in the business.

Family or team?

As a coach gets to know the family business coachee through interviews, observations, narratives, activities and the coaching relationship, it is useful to identify what characteristics they show as a family and as a business team. An example is presented below, using a chart, to distinguish between family and business characteristics. Reflecting on this chart with the coachee can help them identify what works for them as a family and as a business team, what of these can be transferable directly and what needs modification and how. It is also important to discuss potential issues for developing family businesses.

The family business in the example has four members: Hasan the father, Manjit the mother, Divia the daughter and Joshim the son.

The chart below has demonstrated the different critical issues a family as a team and as a business are displaying. You can use this or similar tools to make a record of your observations.

Areas of observation	Family	Team	Potential issues
Leadership	Hasan is the leader. According to the culture they are coming from, the man is the head of the family.	Divia has the clearest vision of what the family business will look like and she has a strong ability to share this vision clearly.	Opportunity: a strategic direction might be formed quicker and easier if Divia is accepted as a leader, even if for a time. Threat: a major clash with the culture the family is from and might have detrimental effect on the family relationships.
Financial decisions	Manjit is solely responsible for managing the family budget.	Hasan is the head of the business and does not share finance decisions but has much less experience with financial management than Manjit.	Opportunity: Hasan and Manjit could share the finance decisions in the business. Threat: the family traditions or operations might be shaken, at least might need renegotiation if Hasan wants to get involved in the family finances as well.

Case study 2: family business coaching with transferable skills

Appendix 7.2 contains a case study to illustrate the transferability of coaching tools from individual coaching to the family business context. A brief description of stages of the coaching process and techniques used in this case is given below.

You will recognise the same techniques that were used in the family business case, supporting our argument that interdisciplinary techniques are easily transferrable and, practitioners' prior knowledge and experience in another discipline substantially contribute to the success of family business coaching.

Summary of case study 2

Margaret wanted to turn her passion into business but was held back by her perceived lack of business skills and apprehension to charge for something she enjoys doing anyway. She contracted a coach to help her develop the business to provide sufficient income enabling her to give up her teaching job. Coaching helped Margaret identify her core values leading her to redefine the coaching objectives to create a business solution that was aligned with her values and was more acceptable and satisfying for her. As a result, Margaret chose to continue working as a teacher, although outside of institutional settings as a private tutor, allowing a more flexible timetable and she established her business part-time that released the pressure on her to generate income solely from her business. In the process she became a confident, astute business person, who discovered how to apply her existing skills and experience into achieving her desired business outcome and work–life balance whilst maintaining her core values.

Coaching intervention: The stages listed below were followed to assist Margaret in achieving her desired outcome.

Stage 1: exploration and contracting

- Exploration of the client's objectives: what do they expect from coaching.
- Exploring and agreeing on what to contract for: what is the source of the problem.

Techniques used: one-to-one interview.

Stage 2: the coaching process

- Identifying the current state and the desired state.
- Identifying core values and how these are maintained in the current state.

- Identifying internal and external resources: creating an inventory of skills and knowledge both on personal and business level, identifying transferability, analysing opportunities, threats, strengths and weaknesses.
- Reflecting: re-enforcing discoveries and learning, how these relate to current problem.
- Planning the road from current state to desired state.
- Taking action.

Techniques used: value elicitation through peak experience, SWOT analysis, stakeholder mapping and management, skills inventory, identification of transferable skills, planning (roadmap).

Stage 3: follow-up evaluation

- Evaluating progress: follow-up on progress at a predefined time point after coaching work completed (six months to one year).

Techniques used: one-to-one interview.

Practical applications: interdisciplinary and transferable skills

Although coaching practices are firmly grounded on psychological models and theories, the coaching practices are also drawing relevant models and approaches from other disciplines. Therefore, to deliver an effective coaching intervention, it is important to explore the application of transferable skills drawn from relevant interdisciplinary subject areas. This section aims to highlight the major processes through which interdisciplinary subject knowledge are transformed into transferable skills for application to family business coaching.

We have provided an example from economics to illustrate the process of bringing relevant knowledge and skills from other relevant disciplines for application to family business coaching. Knowledge about economics and the business market can enhance family business coaching. The coach must use necessary techniques to pull out relevant issues from the family business economy to understand the nature and extent of family business functions. One technique can be a progressive assessment of the economic growth of the family business over the years, and identifying any potential fall in economic returns at any stage of the business operation. Another technique is placing a family business in the balance sheet to measure their strategies to manage demand and supply.

An example is presented below to demonstrate the application of knowledge about economics to facilitate family business coaching.

Progressive assessment of economic growth: family business coaching

	Year one	*Year two*	*Year three*	*Year four*
Overall growth				
Supply				
Demand				
No growth (supply + demand)				

The activities below are bi-functional: they are designed to aid the coach's experiential learning and self-reflection but beyond that they can be integrated into the coach's toolkit for family business coaching.

Skills inventory

This tool helps identify what skills, experiences, learning and observations you have from your professional background, personal life or education and how these can relate to family, business and coaching. Note down your thoughts and ideas and review your skills as you develop in your profession. You might modify the inventory, adding other skills and thinking about their relevance to family business coaching. You also might use the inventory in coaching the family business, either with individual family members or the family working on it together (Appendix 7.3).

SWOT analysis

This is a simple tool to chart Strengths (e.g. what is the competitive advantage over competitors or potential competitors), **Weaknesses** (disadvantage over others), **O**pportunities (what elements of the strengths, circumstances or environment can be exploited to gain advantage) and Threats (elements that can be troublesome or harmful) by drawing a square and four quadrants, a separate one for S.W.O. and T. The tool is typically used in organisations and aids the definition of the organisation's strategy to achieve the expected objectives. SWOT analysis however can be used with family businesses. Performing a SWOT analysis is very simple.

Strengths	Weaknesses
Opportunities	Threats

Looking at your skills inventory (see Appendix 7.1), consider what you would like to develop in your family business coaching practice. List down your SWOTs.

You have now done a SWOT analysis; you have identified the strengths and weaknesses, opportunities and threats. You might have identified areas that you want to familiarise with a bit more and this can open up a new area for your professional development.

You can also use this tool to assess the position of your business on the coaching market. You can use the analysis with your family business coachee just the same way.

Stakeholder mapping and management

It is another simple tool from business management to identify important collaborators and the optimal ways to communicate with them, from a strategic context. It is useful to map all stakeholders according to their power and interests relative to the entity performing the mapping, because it also helps identifying what levels of efforts and what methods are needed to keep them on board. A very simple tool for mapping and stakeholder management planning is presented below. Like with the SWOT analysis, there is no exact science to this; it simply needs thinking through and writing it down with the help of the chart.

	Interest		
Power		**High**	**Low**
	High	Manage closely	Keep satisfied
	Low	Keep informed	Monitor (minimum effort)

Thinking about your family business coaching practice, identify people, organisations, businesses, authorities, groups that would be relevant to the business. Jot them all down on a piece of paper. Then arrange them in the table quadrants by their power to influence the business and how close their interest is in your business. Once you have your stakeholders in the quadrants, think about what kind of relationship or communication you would need to maintain with them. When you have identified the necessary channels of communication and maintaining stakeholder relationships, you can make a future strategic plan for the business. You can offer the same tool to your clients for mapping their stakeholders and defining appropriate management strategies.

Value elicitation using peak experience

Being fully aligned with our values makes us feel good and fulfilled. It is therefore very helpful if you are aware what your core values are and how you can respect them. People however are not always able to clarify their values. One activity to help the clarification process is described below:

- Recall a time when you felt full of energy, absolutely alive, you were fully in the moment, when your body was full of excitement, you even might have thought it was a perfect moment.
- What were you doing? Where were you? Who was around you? What was around you?
- What thoughts/feelings did you have?
- What were the values that you cherished most at that moment?

You might have several thoughts coming to you about what you felt, what your values were. Take a pencil, write it all down. Look at your list again and again, add to it, take away as many times as necessary until you are satisfied you have a list with your core values. Values can typically be described in abstract words, such as love, power, honesty, etc. You might find that your list has words such as money or family which are still not really abstract, if this is the case, think about what values these carry and list the values these things represent. When you have a list of abstract concepts, this is likely to be the list of your core values.

- Think about which parts in your life you have respected these values.
- Where you want to make improvements to develop these values.
- How these changes can be made.

This activity can also be very helpful for your coachee. You can invite them to individually generate a list of their core values and then discuss if these values are shared in the family business. You might also find that there are values shared in the family context that are not necessarily shared in the business context. Discussing these dichotomies and their impact on the business can also help your coachee learn and make an informed decision on what actions they want to take.

Tips for good coaching practice for family businesses with a focus on transferable skills

Some coaches are confident to go to places they have not been before to satisfy their knowledge-seeking behaviour and explore novel ideas and opportunities. Others like to tread more carefully and start with something they know well already and explore new things as they progress. The beauty of family business coaching is that it can be approached from many different angles, thus whatever your strength is, you can put it to the best use. If you are new to family business coaching it might help to look at it in different frames:

Frame 1: A special context in which the family operates—to achieve a certain (set) of objective(s) over a defined period of time.

If your strengths are in the family context, this frame can be the most helpful to you.

A special type of business—where the organisation is predominantly composed of or led by family members. Similarly, to families, all organisations have their own culture, history, and particular individual and team relationships. Families might be slightly, but not significantly different in the private setting than in the business setting, so watch out for these differences.

Frame 2: If you are more comfortable with business coaching, then frame the job as this special case of business coaching.

You might have a particular expertise or more experience in one area of coaching. Using the above examples of framing, find the most suitable frame that gives you a familiar ground to start your engagement. Examples might be team coaching, leadership coaching, career coaching, developmental coaching, life coaching, etc.

Although family business coaching can be very rewarding, it can also be fairly challenging because you are not only dealing with one individual, a group or team in an organisational context, but a group of individuals who have a special connection outside of the business context. In the family setting, this same group of people might function optimally with dynamics, structure, roles or members' identities different from what is necessary for the business to flourish. Family roles, family members' identities, family structure and dynamics most probably had evolved and existed long before the family business coaching commenced; therefore, the conscious or unconscious resistance to change might be stronger than in a setting where there is no special relationship between the group/team members outside of the organisational context.

Using experience from our own families, we might find that our coachee's family presents issues, conflicts, experiences that are familiar to us from our own experiences. Because of this familiarity it is easy to be drawn in emotionally and lose our objectivity.

Frame 3: Self-reflexivity, the art of continuously observing and noting our feelings, thoughts, behaviours, and understanding their origin and effect in a given context, is one of the three fundamental assets that make a professional coach.

Professional supervision is a practice that ensures our reflective learning, identifies our professional gaps and helps to maintain our conscious efforts to remain within the boundaries of our professional competencies to provide the best assistance to our coachees and refraining from causing harm.

Frame 4: Both self-reflexivity and supervision are essential elements of the continuous professional development, the drive and practice to keep learning and evolving our knowledge and ourselves as professionals.

Conclusion

The contribution of interdisciplinary approaches to family business coaching is apparent in practical application. These approaches are serving as rich platforms on which transferable skills are developed to apply to family business coaching. The importance of formalising and applying knowledge from interdisciplinary subject areas to coaching family businesses is highlighted and the need for coaching practitioners to develop personal and professional skills in a range of related and relevant subject areas is emphasised in this chapter. This will not only provide depth in the coaching practice but also the breadth and integrated approach in the practical application of discipline-focused coaching practice. The demand for tools and techniques in family business coaching can be met by using interdisciplinary knowledge and approaches. We have provided a few examples in this chapter, and we encourage all coaching practitioners to utilise their existing knowledge repertoire of different disciplines to develop and advance integrated interdisciplinary coaching practices for the family businesses. Coaching psychology is informed by knowledge and ideas of different related disciplines. The effective coaching intervention can be achieved with appropriate appreciation of the contributions of related disciplines. In this chapter, we have argued in favour of relevant and related interdisciplinary knowledge and practical applications to deliver successful coaching outcomes for family businesses.

References

Allen, K. (2013). A framework for family life coaching. *International Coaching Psychology Review, 8*(1): 72–79.

Berne, E. (1964). *Games People Play*. New York, NY: Grove Press, Inc.

Grant, M. A. (2006). Workplace and executive coaching: A bibliography from the scholarly business literature. In: R. Stober & A. M. Grant (Eds.), *Evidence Based*

Coaching Handbook. Putting Best Practices to Work for Your Clients, (pp. 367–388). Hoboken, NJ: Wiley.

Goldenberg, I., & Goldenberg, H. (2004). *Family Therapy: An Overview*. Pacific Grove, CA: Brookes/Cole.

Handy, C. B. (1976). *Understanding Organizations*. New York, NY: Oxford University Press.

Parker, P., Hall, D. T., & Kram, K. E. (2008). Peer coaching: A relational process for accelerating career learning. *Academy of Management Learning & Education, 7*: 487–503.

Salovey, P., & Mayer, J. (1990). Emotional intelligence. *Imagination, Cognition and Personality, 9*: 185–211.

Segers, J., Vloeberghs, D., & Henderickx, E. (2011). Structuring and understanding the coaching industry: The coaching cube. *Academy of Management Learning & Education, 10*: 204–221.

Schein, E. (1992). *Organisational Culture and Leadership: A Dynamic View*. San Francisco, CA: Josey-Bass.

Shams, M. (2006). Approaches in business coaching; exploring context-specific and cultural issues. In: M. Shams & P. Jackson (Eds.), *Developments in Work and Organizational Psychology* (pp. 229–244). The Netherlands: Elsevier.

Shams, M. (2011). Recent developments in family business coaching. In: M. Shams & D. Lane (Eds.), *Coaching in the Family Owned Business: A Path to Growth* (pp. 13–20). London: Routledge.

Appendices

Appendix 7.1: Case study 1

Family business: Eve and Steve

Eve and Steve were the owners of a small health service business. Most of their working life, they were public sector professionals but close to retirement global economic downturn forced to set up their own business. The business was expected to provide for the rest of their lives, including retirement years throughout which they planned to keep working. Neither had business acumen nor did they have any experience in setting up, managing or running a business, but they had a bit of capital that they invested in the new business—a healthcare centre in the annex of their large family home, with several fully equipped consultation rooms.

After two years, their financial position was dire and they had to tap into their life savings to keep the business running despite a fairly steady and satisfied clientele. It was obvious that something had to be done.

Apart from Eve and Steve, two of their grown-up children, also healthcare professionals, were registered as part-time employees in the business. The other employee was a full-time highly specialist administrator.

The children were fairly inactive in the business, and they have not contributed to the running costs.

The coaching contract was with Eve and Steve to enable them turning their business sustainable and to generate enough income to live on. Their children agreed to be involved in the coaching process to a limited extent. The pre-coaching sessions involved one-to-one interviews with all family members to understand their individual perceptions of the situation, their expectations of the coaching process and their agendas, including alignment with and differences from the contracted coaching outcome. These sessions revealed that the traditional family roles and behaviours were unconsciously carried over to the business setting. The parents did not want to burden the children with their problems and never talked about them in-depth. They wanted to provide a safe and comfortable environment for when the children will need to use the business for their progress. The children chose to take the children's position and remain oblivious to the problems (*understanding the concept of transactional analysis* was useful here, observing the apparent lack of Adult–Adult transactions between parents and children). The children only vaguely engaged with the business. So here was a business frame in which the family continued to function as a family and there were a lot of unspoken words (*or hidden agendas*). But there was a lot of love and care in the family too.

In the first family session, the coach asked the family to discuss an experience they all shared and that was a very nice memory for everybody. They retold how they liked to go hiking with the children when the children were little, the fun they had discovering beautiful things together.

Using a positive memory that was seemingly far from the doom of the business was a good starting position. Reliving positive experiences can help enter into a positive, hopeful, joyful and more creative cognitive and emotional state that might aid finding new ways of approaching a problem. It was important to observe and reinforce the positive physiological states and joyful and resourceful language used in these narratives. It was also useful to anchor these positive states and create a catalogue of the combined family resources emerging from these memories. These could be called upon when problem states were entered into and could be checked for transferability.

The narrative also revealed the family members' individual strengths and weaknesses, and it was discussed which ones can be transferred (*using a family and business characteristics comparison*) to create opportunities and which ones mean threats to the family business (*applying SWOT analysis*) and what can be done to address these.

The family peak experience helped identify core values that family members unanimously shared, such as love, family, caring, sharing, trust (*Value elicitation through peak experience*). It was then discussed how these values could be shared and honoured in the business context, what the business would look like honouring the core values, and in this way the vision for the business was drafted. Using a clear objective, the family has together created a strategy, the "roadmap" to get to the state of desired outcome and identified what needed to change to get there. Creating an inventory of resources (*using a tool based on the skills inventory*) has furthered the family to clearly identify what resources they had in-house, what were those they would have had to acquire or buy and what were not essential to achieve their objectives, even though they thought them important initially.

A crucial step was the identification of transferable skills from all family members, for example, Eve struggled to see how she could get the business run on a shoestring budget until she recalled how she had to manage the young family on a very tight budget as a mother. Then she realised that the same skills and experience were applicable in the business context. The family also realised that when they were hiking, even though the children were small, everybody had their own area of responsibility and everybody took part in decisions, small or big. Drawing parallels from that experience to the present business context led to the realisation that the children were not given responsibilities in the business even though they would have been capable of taking part in decision-making and could fulfil their part.

These discoveries have led to restructuring the business, making confident saving decisions with all the members involved and reconfiguring areas of responsibility building on strengths of the individuals and of the entire team. The children, for example, developed a competitive price list and included the cost of maintaining the business—an idea Eve and Steve never contemplated: their pricing so far had been emotionally driven, they did not want to charge "too much" to their clients.

A follow-up evaluation a year after the coaching contract ended confirmed that the business achieved sustainability by generating a steady income and keeping the costs manageable. Family members equally contributed to the business both in terms of income generation and in monitoring the business performance, taking business decisions as necessary. Eve and Steve could generate enough income to live on and they did not have to draw from their savings any more. Eve and Steve also reported that the family communication outside the business has also changed and there were many more Adult–Adult conversations after they applied the learning and experiences from the family business coaching.

Appendix 7.2: Case study 2

Margaret was a semi-retired school teacher and was thinking about setting up her own business, making celebration cakes. All her friends and family had been commissioning cakes from her for years. Margaret would have liked to have stopped working altogether and earn a living from her cake making but she did not know how. She did not think she had any business skills and she felt she should not have been paid for something she enjoyed doing anyway. On the other hand, if she did not start to earn from cake making, she would have needed to give it up completely and find something else to get income from as the family finances turned dire after her husband recently retired.

When Margaret talked about what was important for her in the cake making, she showed the physiological signs of reliving a peak experience and she indeed said that she is experiencing the state of "flow" when making her cakes: she does not notice time passing and is completely absorbed in the activity. Margaret identified the values associated with this experience as giving love, compassion, making others happy, creativity (*using value elicitation through peak experience, which is similar to the technique in Case study 1*). Margaret then reflected on how much she was living by these values (*this can also be used in the family business coaching context, that is, asking the members how much the family values are lived by in the business*). In her teaching career Margaret very much maintained her core values. Realising this, Margaret discovered that cake making was becoming a substitute for her teaching where indirectly she could provide love, compassion, happiness, creativity that she would be missing when retiring from teaching. This realisation has modified the desired outcome of the coaching because Margaret decided that she wanted to continue teaching by giving private tuition and earn modestly from cake making too (*It is a general coaching principle to remain flexible and renegotiate the coaching objective in line with your client's learning and development*).

Completing the skills inventory, the "business part for use without prior business experience", Margaret emerged much more confident and reflected on areas of her future business as to where and how she could utilise her existing skills. The coaching involved application of *SWOT analysis, stakeholder mapping and management, and these have helped* Margaret to create *a roadmap* to address the questions as listed in the *"business management"* section.

At the end of the coaching, Margaret had a clear vision of her future businesses, that is, private tuition and cake making. She identified her strengths and the areas she would need to ask others to help in setting up her business (e.g. building a website with professional photos of her cakes). She also developed a plan to promote her cake business (by personal recommendation) and established how much she may need to earn to keep her business developing at a level comfortable to her. She has emerged as a confident small business owner being in control of her business affairs.

Appendix 7.3: Skills inventory

Please review the topics and think of what you know about these. You might have first-hand experience, might have observed or might have learned about these topics. This set of activities is designed to help you identify transferable skills for elements of business management. They can be used both for the coach's own business and as aids in coaching the family business.

Skill/experience	Own (lived) experience	Observed through others	Taught/ read about it	Notes and thoughts
Business—use this inventory sheet if you HAVE business experience				
Identifying stakeholders: clients, suppliers, supporters, sponsors				
Understanding clients' needs				
Product specification				
Marketing				
Analysis/understanding of market				
Understanding suppliers needs				
Leadership in business				
Organisational culture				
Mapping key contacts				
Managing stakeholders				
Formulating strategy				
Identifying competitors				
Formulating vision				
Planning for success				
Monitoring progress				
Proactive contingency planning				
add your own				

Skill/experience business—use this inventory sheet if you DO NOT have business experience	Activity	Notes and thoughts
	Think of something that you would like to achieve, for example, a trip, a work goal or anything else that is important to you.	
Identify your resources: what do you have to offer?	Take a piece of paper and a pen. Write down everything that you are good at, skills, knowledge, experiences, expertise, talents: your own "internal resources" or "strengths" and material things you can offer or trade in to achieve your goal: your "material resources" or "assets". Try to find 20–25 each. This will be your "resource inventory"	
Identify important people around *you* who can help: family members, friends, work contacts, friends of friends, colleagues, people who can help your enterprise.	Draw a circle in the middle of a paper, that's you. Draw circles for all the people and connections you have who might help you in whatever you want to achieve.	
Understand suppliers' needs: who can help me and why are they helping?	Identify and add to this sheet who would help *you* and why. What would they want in return, or how can you help them? Include people and organisations who you need to liaise with (e.g. bank, council) and those you need to buy something from (goods or services).	
Mapping key contacts: who are around me?	Now you have a "map" of all your contacts for what you want to achieve. Mark the most important people and organisations in this "map".	

Understanding other people's (clients') needs: what do you really need from me?	List five examples of how you understand what others (family members, colleagues, friends, even strangers you met) need from you.	
Product specification: what is it I am having?	Look back at your resource inventory—identify your ten strongest resources: your most eminent strengths or assets for this.	
Marketing: what is it I am having that you need?	List an example for each of your ten most eminent strengths or assets for how you used them in the past for someone who needed exactly this from you.	
Analysis/ understanding of the market: who needs what I am having? who else is having it or something very similar and how do I differ?	Name someone you know personally or who you follow, for each of your eminent strengths who also has these. Identify how they are similar/different from you, what you can learn from them and what they could learn from you.	
Leadership in business	Write down examples of leaders, good and bad. They might be your own experience (work, school, scouts) or someone you observed in politics, history, etc. Identify what makes them good and bad leaders for you. What would the bad leaders need to change to become good? What changes would make the good leaders bad? Please note: there is no right or wrong answer; it is about what a good leader is for *you*.	
Organisational culture	Think about groups, families, groups of friends you know. How can you describe them by something they have in common? Do they use certain expressions? Can they be described by how they dress? Do they have stories they share? Do they have shared beliefs? Do they have shared values they hold?	

Managing stakeholders	Think about a situation or area of your life. List down all contacts that are relevant to it, from authorities (e.g. utilities) through shops (e.g. where you buy your groceries) to your family or friends as applicable. How do you need to communicate with them in respect of this situation or area of your life? What do they need to know? What are the differences between them in what they need to know? What causes these differences?	
Formulating strategy: how to get where I want to be.	Think about something simple you want to accomplish, for example, doing the weekly shopping. How are you going to do this? Can you draw up an outline of completing this task from start to finish?	
Identifying competitors	Look back at your resource inventory and your most eminent strengths. Think about who else has them. How are you different from them? In what aspects are you stronger? In what aspects are you weaker?	
Formulating vision	Think about something you want to realise in the future, for example, a dream holiday. Write down in as much detail as possible how this will look like, where it will be, who will be there, what will it sound, feel, smell like, what noises, voices will be there. Visualise as vividly as you can. If you cannot see it, feel it with your other senses and list these experiences.	

Monitoring progress	Think about something simple you want to accomplish, for example, your weekly shopping. Think about what signs and actions you will identify that things are being on the right track to accomplish this task by the time you wanted and within the conditions you wanted.	
Planning ahead for a possible crisis	Think about the steps that you will have to take for this above task. What can go wrong? What can happen unexpectedly? How can you prevent that? If you cannot prevent, how can you remedy what went wrong?	
add your own		

When you finished working on an inventory activity, a selection of activities or the complete skills inventory (it's up to you what chunks you take as working units), reflect on how you are going to use these skills in your business.

Chapter 8

Coaching competency indicators and coaching performance appraisal

Manfusa Shams and Dasha Grajfoner

Introduction

Family businesses are contributing to a high percentage (90 per cent) of the national economy all around the world (Mattioli, 2009). As such there is a growing interest for family business coaching to provide sustainable support for the families in a business context. Family business coaching requires a unique set of business and personal coaching skills such as, knowledge about group dynamics, communication and relationships issues, conflict, emotionally charged issues, ownership and generational influences on the business function. We need to add a few new elements in this pandemic. This relates to the new way of working by the family business and the coaching practitioners. This new way of performing business can be stressful to a family business as this requires advanced training and coordinated teamwork. In addition, personal health and safety issues need to be prioritised to adhere to the lockdown restrictions, social distancing and restricted mobility options.

A few research generated from the pandemic effects on businesses has highlighted the positive consequences of this pandemic. This relates to the growing interests to implement advanced cutting-edge technology in business operations and delivery, and gaining relevant experiences to achieve competitive advantage (Akpan et al., 2020). A coaching practitioner needs to develop skills and competencies to deliver the coaching needs of a family business in the context of this pandemic. However, it is also important to identify generic cognitive and performance-based skills, competencies for an effective coaching intervention to support the standard coaching needs prior to the delivery of a pandemic-driven coaching intervention.

The focus in this chapter is therefore to present challenges that family business coaching practitioners are facing to self-assess their own performance using relevant tools and techniques and to plan the development of relevant skills (PD) to facilitate effective deliveries of coaching interventions.

The need for assessments and evidence-based practice is arising from the demand for professional and personal development of coaching practitioners to deliver competent and efficient coaching interventions for the benefit of

DOI: 10.4324/9781003174721-8

family businesses irrespective of business types, lengths of businesses, and family dynamics (Shams, 2011).

Typically, a coach is engaged in self-assessment using evaluation measures from the coaching practice, peer-assessment, supervision, self-monitored checklist and the success rate of coaching outcomes. These measures are applied to all types of coaching irrespective of any specific measure needed for any coaching approach. For example, family business coaching may demand specific measures as the practice is built on a blended coaching approach—coaching a family and a business simultaneously (Shams, 2011).

As coaching competencies relevant for family-based business interventions tap into both personal and business coaching, a coach may have to integrate various areas of coaching: couples, family and group coaching, mediation, relationship, personal and team coaching. This requires a broad set of skills. It is not uncommon that the need for addressing negotiation, conflict resolution, communication, and personal *vs.* business interests appears to surface during the coaching sessions and as coaching interventions progress. Family business coaching, therefore, calls for a complex set of skills to address any unexpected issues during the coaching sessions. A crucial competency, however, is the ability to recognise the required skills, and engage other experts should that be necessary.

In this chapter, we are arguing for a collective approach to address performance-related challenges family business coaches are frequently facing, and the need for research evidence and policies to develop performance-related assessments and competencies indicators for family business coaching practitioners.

Key questions

- What are the major performance-related skills a coach must have to deliver effective family business coaching interventions?
- What type of competency is required for a coach to bring successful outcomes for a family business?
- What is performance-related assessment in a coaching context and how the assessment is carried out?
- What does a coaching psychologist need to do to gain professional blended skills (family and business) to coach family businesses?
- What are the indicators for effective performance in coaching practice and how can continuing professional development and supervision help to achieve competencies and efficiency in performance?

We have addressed each key question using the following subheadings. The discussion in each of these sections is expected to demonstrate a common thread, that is, understanding coaching competency indicators and performance-related assessments for the coaching practitioners. Although our discussion is predominantly focused on family business coaching, however, we hope the critical discussions will support the need for measuring relevant coaching competencies and performance-related assessments for all coaching practices to ensure effective coaching interventions and successful coaching outcomes.

Specific performance-related issues for a family business coach

Family-run businesses represent a substantial part of economy. In coaching practice, we often encounter a family business initiated by a family member, who leads the business, sets the leadership strategy and organisational values. Specific coaching issues depend on how long the business has been operating and its stage of development.

Some of the most common coaching issues in new family businesses are lack of identity, vision and long-term goals. This is an important area, and the family businesses normally do not invest in coaching for market recognition, leadership, vision, and succession. The question of leadership in family business is as equally important as in other organisations. However, due to family ties, the coach should expect a variety of issues that can interfere in the coaching process: lack of clear division between work and family life, personal attachment to the organisation by the founder, poor communication and generational differences between the founders and successors. These intergenerational issues may result in the lack of interest in potential successors—paired with increased ownership of the founder.

Establishing strong brand identity and its position on the market is important for dealing with the competition from either multinational companies or other family businesses. Ineffective or lack of communication, poor listening skills, different values and preferences, unclear roles, lack of organisational identity are just some of the issues frequently encountered in a family business coaching practice.

The main issues can therefore be summarised as follows:

* Managing change (succession planning, letting go).
* Communications skills (conflict resolution, mediation skills).
* Balancing business and personal relations (ability to differentiate between family and business issues, stress management, time management).
* Clarity of roles (including leadership in various areas).
* Personal relationships (mutual respect, appreciation, etc.).

The following case study has illustrated a common setup and an array of issues in a family business that a coach might encounter.

Case study 1

Steve is a 59-year-old owner of a small hospitality business, he started when he was thirty. His main reasons to see the coaching psychologist were declining business paired with conflicts he had on a regular basis with his wife and two sons, who also worked in his business. He felt that the business suffered due to their poor working relations.

The coach decided to start with the GROW model to explore the reality of the coachee and used Socratic questioning to clarify various issues the coachee is dealing with.

In the first session, the coachee explained his daily schedule and he soon came to a realisation that there was a lack of work-family life balance. Steve spent 16 hours a day working. He had his vision on how the business should run and felt that his family members were primarily his employees. This is a good example of work and family life imbalance because Steve did not invest an equal amount of time with his family.

In subsequent sessions, the coachee explored the balance between his business and personal relationships.

The coachee clearly showed some awareness of the problems associated with unsuccessful balancing family and business and his perception of family members at the beginning of coaching process. The coach attempted to further increase the awareness of the impact the situation had on the coachee and his family, using questions like: How is this affecting you and your wife/sons? How do you feel about this now when you have explained how you and your family are affected by the situation?

Simple Socratic questions are used to encourage the awareness of thinking patterns, feelings, and associated behaviours. By the end of the first session, it became clear that there was a complexity of issues related to balancing family and business relationships, poor communication, resentment from all sides, unresolved personal and business conflicts, lack of respect; and from business side, they were not working as a team due to poor leadership, lack of mutually agreed vision and clarity of roles.

A fragment from the dialogues between the coach and the coachee is presented below:

Case study 1: dialogues between a coach and coachee

Coach: How do you see the balance between your business and family relationship with your wife and two sons?
Coachee: I work long hours, so I predominantly see my wife and sons as my employees. Do not get me wrong, I love them, but my personal relationships are almost gone if I think about it ... You see, my business is my life and

I sometimes cannot understand why my family does not see my business in the same way.

The client clearly shows here some awareness of the problems associated with unsuccessful balancing of family and business and his perception of family members. The coach attempted to further increase the awareness of the impact the situation had on the client and his family, using questions like: How is this affecting you and your wife/sons? How do you feel about this now when you have explained how you and your family are affected by the situation?

Learning from the case study

*   Family business coaching in this case calls for a blended approach.
*   Personal and business relations are clearly intertwined.
*   The issues are complex and must be addressed appropriately.
*   The coach rightfully resorts to more existential approaches.

This case study highlights the complexity that a family business coach is facing and it indicates relevant coaching competencies required, for example, communication coaching, existential or personal construct coaching to explore values or preferences between generations, strategic coaching to clearly define work and family roles, positive psychology and cognitive behavioural coaching to increase motivation, leadership coaching and goal setting.

This complexity calls for a blended approach, where the coach demonstrates an integration of skills used: careful case formulation, weighting of family or personal and business coaching, decisions about the theoretical framework used—sometimes the framework will be integrative, sometimes a behavioural technique like GROW model will be more appropriate. Overall the coach does not need just an ability, experience and knowledge to deal with different areas of coaching and jump from leadership coaching to personal coaching and mediation, but also be able to pull out a relevant underlying theoretical model to justify their application in an intervention. The coach in this case correctly explored Steve's reality to assess the complexity of the issues and made attempts to increase coachees' awareness.

The main feature of this case study is the use of strategic coaching and personal construct coaching. Strategic coaching refers to the exploration of various tools and techniques with the coachee to determine the most suitable tools for application. In family-based businesses, this is often a necessary step due to complexity of the issues. The other aspect of strategic coaching is the awareness of the organisational culture, which in family business often reflects social culture and personal values that are influenced by it. Therefore, strategic coaching explores the organisational culture and the coach manifests leadership competencies by reshaping the strategy or the culture of the organisation. Personal construct coaching refers to the exploration of personal and organisational constructs. These constructions refer to the coachee, the other members of the business, and the family. Two activities are proposed to illustrate strategic and personal construct coaching's below.

Activity for strategic coaching: mission statement

- Composing individual and team strategic plans for your practice.
- Which generic and specific competencies are present in my strategic plan and what can I do to develop the ones that are missing?

Each member of the team is asked to come up with the best mission statement for the organisation. They can be asked to provide a mission statement that describes the organisation at the moment, and an ideal mission statement, that would reflect a future business shaped by them.

These mission statements are then used in one-to-one and team coaching to achieve commonly agreed values that will then influence the strategy and the culture within the family business.

This exercise can be done with one or a group of coachees.

Activity for personal construct coaching

- Personal and work core values and beliefs.
- How are these values and beliefs reflected in my own practice?
- Which generic and specific competencies are reflecting my own core values?

Each business/family member is asked to come up with their values that are important to them in their personal and work life. The coachees are encouraged to elicit as many values as possible. In the next stage the coachees are asked to choose a certain number of most important values for them—in their work and their family life. These are often core values that have to be present in order for the coachee to feel valued and appreciated. The family and business values may overlap or they might be identical.

Working with all members of a family business can help to identify the core values of each member with an aim to compare and to see how much they do overlap.

Coaching competencies

A family business setup is a specific environment, hence coaching interventions may require a wide set of competencies. These competencies can be categorised as generic and specific, and we have presented the significant features of these competencies and their relevance to a family business.

Generic competencies

Generic competencies are those that should be acquired by any coach or coaching psychologist practitioner. These include the awareness of psychological evidence, ethical guidelines adopted by the professional organisation, knowledge and understanding of coaching techniques, approaches and theoretical frameworks. Some coaches may be trained to use a particular model or technique. This could be useful in some situations but not all. Therefore, one of the most important general competencies is to assess one's own skills and ability to deal with the case. If the coach is operating within one model or technique, there has to be full awareness of the evidence that this approach is based on. The coach also needs an awareness of the limitations of the approach. Therefore, exercising and understanding the link between the coaching issue, client's needs and expectations, and coaching practitioner's own competencies is crucial. Ideally, a reflective practitioner model is employed in many instances to address this competency issue.

The coach or coaching psychologist must have good communication skills that include listening skills, an ability to clearly convey information to the client with verbal and non-verbal communication. This information could take the form of listening, acceptance, guidance, empathy, and leadership. One of the important outcomes of this is an engaging coaching process. The coachee's engagement, therefore, depends on a coaching practitioner's degree of motivation and communication skills. This engagement is one of the performance indicators that we will look at later.

In the above case study, the coach clearly provides a safe and empathic space for the coachee, whilst exploring his reality and further possibilities.

Due to a mix of personal and business issues, family businesses are inherently dealing with personal issues even though they are wrapped into business matters. These personal topics can become emotional and the coach has to be able to handle those, sometimes difficult, emotional situations. The coach here has to provide a strong guidance and perhaps a certain degree of leadership.

All these generic competencies underline the basic competencies relevant for a family business coach, the basic competencies integrate both business and personal coaching skills. These basic competencies are coach's ability to explain the coaching process that is relevant for both business and personal coaching. The coach has to be able to highlight the relationship between these two areas to the coachee and explain possible conflicts. The coach needs skills to build, maintain, and explore the coaching relationship, even when addressing difficult issues. These difficult issues normally stem from the personal relationships between the business owners or owners and the employees. In the process of building and maintaining a coaching relationship, the coach has to be able to work with the clients to achieve the coaching goals that were mutually agreed.

Specific competencies

Specific competencies relevant for family business coaching refer to management skills and the ability to guide the coachee to set and maintain a coaching plan. At the early stages of the coaching process increasing awareness of a coachee's own action, thinking, and feelings are most important. Due to the specificity of the family business setup, the business part of the competencies should include good knowledge and understanding of family business structure and context. There should be a good understanding of the social and organisational culture that contextualise family business. Depending on the cultural background of the business, the coach needs to demonstrate a good understanding of leadership, not only to include it in the coaching process but also to self-reflect on their guidance. Often family businesses will expect from the coach to take on an arbitrary role. Due to blended personal and business components, the coaching intervention can be challenging and the coach has to employ self-reflection, peer or general supervision to self-assess their performances.

The generic and specific competencies are closely interrelated and a coaching intervention may require both applications. The choice is subjected to a coach's understanding of, and ability to assess the needs of the family business under coaching intervention. Because of the complexity, the coach should have the space to reflect on their own, with their peer and during supervision sessions. Working as reflective practitioners, the coach's ability to link their coaching practice to psychology-based evidence is paramount.

Table 8.1 summarises the major elements in generic and specific competencies.

Table 8.1 Major elements in generic and specific coaching competencies

Generic competencies	Specific competencies
Knowledge and understanding awareness of ethics, professional standards	Engagement with the coaching family-centred coaching approach and guidance
Communication skills and information processing	Knowledge depth in family dynamics
Leadership and interpersonal relations	Interface between family and business—insights
Time management	Social context and business history

Applications of relevant competencies: case study 1

The coach has demonstrated the use of generic and specific competencies. Generic competencies were demonstrated in linking the case formulation and the use of GROW as a model with psychology-based evidence. The coach has followed the ethical guidelines, including confidentiality and acquired consent to share the information in supervision sessions, and finally demonstrated an eclectic choice of coaching techniques and tools. Steve was provided with guidance in a safe and empathic environment. Case formulation included lack of motivation, lack of vision and clear goals. The coach proceeded with exploring long-term vision with Steve.

By using tools like Socratic questions, the coach has demonstrated good communication skills. At the end of the sessions, the coachee has reported being more aware of the issues in his family business. He has also reported that he felt he was being listened to in a long time and he was also reported being positively challenged to reflect on the past and think about the future of his company and his own role in that company. The coach guided Steve and therefore demonstrated leadership, guidance and empathy. The client and his family got involved in the process. The coach managed to sustain clients' engagement for the duration of the coaching process, which lasted about six months, consisting of seven sessions. Separate coaching sessions were organised for other family members and two sessions were joint. In the joint sessions, the coach has used the same principles as in organisational team or group coaching. One of the stumbling blocks when working with the family as a group was the lack of acknowledging previous joint achievements and too much focus on the problems and shortcomings of the other person. Here the coach has included the elements of mediation and conflict resolution as well as cognitive behavioural and positive psychology coaching.

The group sessions started with identifying the problems, continued with mediation and conflict resolution. The final stages of the group coaching included shared vision, goals and planning of their personal and business life as a group.

Competencies demonstrated here by the coach are good knowledge of different approaches and coaching techniques. Generic competencies are demonstrated in regular supervision and peer supervision sessions on which some of the issues were discussed in full confidence. Her case formulation, which included the lack of motivation, lack of vision, and clear goals were discussed during supervisions.

Performance-related assessment: coaching practice

Coaches are standing up for demonstrating excellent leadership qualities to guide their coachees, as such their own performance and related behaviours, emotional intelligence, efficacy, etc. are under scrutiny continuously. A coach also has to adjust and adapt to the environment in which coaching is carried out and also in respect to their coachee's responses (Walach-Bista, 2013). According to Chelladurai's (1978) Multidimensional Model of Leadership in Sport, effectiveness of coaching behaviour is the result of interplay between a coach's behaviour and various contextual factors. Since then a number of research has addressed contextual factors affecting coaching practices (Shams, 2006), but less attention is paid to the measures used to facilitate a coach's performance and performance-related assessment both during and after the coaching sessions. For example, coaching educational experience is highly significantly related to coaching efficacy than coaching context (Sullivan, Paquette, Holt & Bloom, 2012), and this implies that performance-related assessments in a coaching context must take into account all personal and socio-demographic factors of a coach. The importance of a coach's behaviour to the effective delivery of a coaching intervention was evident in the following statement, "Coaching behaviours do 'not occur in a vacuum'; rather contextual factors 'lead up to', or explain, the types of behaviours that coaching practitioners will exhibit in sport setting" (Horn, 2008, pp. 243–244). A good and ethically driven coaching practice therefore must consider the complex inter-relationships between a coachee's behaviour, personal factors of a coachee and a coach, socio-economic and other contextual factors encompassing the coaching practice for a family business. Culture is an important part of this process. Family business is influenced by culture more so than a non-family organisation. Cultural and generational values will be manifested in a family business (Shams, 2006). Therefore, the coach has to be aware and familiar with cultural as well as developmental coaching issues.

Blended approach to assess performance: family business coaching

Family business coaching involves a blended approach in which equal attention should be paid to coach a family as well as their business with a focus on interdependency between them (Shams, 2011). As such, assessment of coaching performance requires dual but integrated assessment approach—assessing coaching performance for family-related issues/family dynamics and assessing coaching performance for business issues. There is no published evidence on assessing family business coaching performance. However, the need to assess coaching behaviour remains (Sullivan, Paquette, Holt & Bloom, 2012), and this also applies to family business coaching performance. We are using mutually exclusive terms, coaching behaviour and coaching performance, in our discussion here. Family business coaching demands careful scrutiny of a coach's behaviour because the coach deals with private and confidential issues of a family, and this requires the use of an integrated interdisciplinary approach, special tools and techniques. For example, family therapy/coun-selling in conjunction with other specific types of coaching (e.g. leadership, solution-focused) is tailored to meet the needs of a family business. The case study below is demonstrating the complexities involving the application of a blended approach.

Case study 2

Jay's family runs a family business in India. They provide internationally accredited courses and have grown their business significantly over the past few years. The business was started by Jay's grandfather, who is still involved and sits on the Board of Directors. Regardless of their success Jay has started questioning his commitment to the business, which worries his family as they all depend on the business. His parents, who are employed by the company, feel stressed and anxious; so does Jay's wife.

The coach was called in by Jay's grandfather, who asked the coach to help Jay to get reasonable. Jay recently started spending more time in the gym and has disconnected from the family and the business.

Jay was reluctant about the coaching sessions but agreed to see the coach nevertheless.

After the initial session, the coach did a case formulation. As Jay was questioning his position in the family and in their business the coach decided to start with exploring Jay's core values. The coach decided not to explore goals, but rather explore Jay's core constructs.

At the start of the process the coach explored Jay's thoughts and feelings about coaching. Jay responded very positively and showed an interest in exploring different options. By doing this he became more enthusiastic about being a part of his family business.

The detailed dialogues between the coach and the coachee are presented here:

Dialogue between a coach and a coachee

Coach: Jay, I can see that you are a bit reluctant to start with the coaching sessions. How do you feel being in the session?

Coachee: It is actually ok. I was a bit resentful as I felt my family tried to force me to get back to the business without actually exploring what I want. I kind of fell into this position without having the time to see what else is out there.

Coach: Are you saying that if you had a chance to explore other avenues you would be happier to continue with the family business.

Coachee: Yes, perhaps. I am not saying that I am not happy or that I want to explore other things, but I am not really sure who am I in this picture and even though everyone is expecting me to be in this role, I am not sure how this role fits me.

Coach: Providing that I am here, would you like to continue with the sessions and how do you think you could benefit from coaching?

Coachee: Yes, it seems that this could be very useful, just to find myself and to clarify what I want from life. I think this would be a sensible thing to do for me and for my family, as I do not want to let them down.

Learning from the case study

- Generic and specific competencies were used.
- The importance of case formulation.
- Blended approach is most suitable.
- Existential and constructivist coaching are more relevant than goal setting.
- Mixing the approaches and techniques will bring effective outcomes.

After a couple of sessions, the coach explored the reality of the client, using parts of the GROW model and Socratic questions. The coach has first explored whether a behavioural approach was appropriate but found out it was not so useful after taking Jay's responses into consideration. As a consequence, the coach decided to use personal construct psychology coaching (Kelly, 1955) and explore Jay's construction system. A Repertory grid technique (Fransella et al., 2004) was also used and this consists of three stages:

a   Elicitation of constructs.
b   Further clarification.
c   Scoring.
   i   In the elicitation stage the clients are encouraged to come up with different bipolar constructs that describe people they work with or their family members. The elicitation is most effective if asked to compare how similar or different those family/business members are.
   ii   Clarification of the constructs helps the coach to understand the meaning behind the words and to identify core and peripheral constructs.
   iii   The final stage enables the client to score each person on his/her core constructs.

By using the repertory grid technique both the coach and the coachee can get a better understanding of the coachee's construction system, including the core values and their perception of the complexity that is inherent to family-owned businesses. An example of the application of repertory grid technique is presented in Appendix 8.1.

Jay had six coaching sessions using personal construct psychology and repertory grid technique. After the fourth session, the coach and Jay had very clear picture about Jay's values, preferences, core and peripheral constructs.

As he was very unsure about his future plans before, Jay felt his sense of self-identity was clearer and having better awareness of himself he could position himself in the family and the family business. The next step for Jay was simple goal setting. However, those goals were always referred back to Jay's core values and constructs. The same approach was used with three other key family members. After the process was completed, the coach organised three group-coaching sessions with all four clients. At those sessions they looked at their shared core values and constructs and they clarified the roles they wanted to take within the family business. One of the main parameters was that the roles were congruent with their values and constructs. The family business went on, Jay stayed and is now the CEO of the company.

Learning from the case study

- The importance of existential and constructivist approaches when suitable.
- The case formulation directs the approaches and tools used.
- One-to-one as well as team coaching skills are necessary.

The coach in this case has demonstrated case formulation skills and her ability to look at the bigger picture, that is, context. A few coaching sessions were done with other key family and business members. As Jay was seen as the main "problematic" person, the coach started with exploring Jay's identity and core constructs. At the later stage she used the same approach with other key members.

After the case formulation, the coach explored which coaching approach would be best suited for Jay. As Jay appeared to first be in a conflict in himself in regards to what the family expects from him and his commitment to the family and family business, and his own aspirations as an individual, the coach decided to try two approaches: behaviouristic and personal construct psychology. The first would enable Jay to go out, explore, try and test different things. However, it soon became clear that Jay was asking more existential questions and was trying to "find himself and his role" as he puts it. Therefore, the coach decided that personal construct psychology coaching with repertory grid technique would be more useful.

The coach has demonstrated that she has an overview of behavioural and personal construct approaches, understands theoretical bases and is able to link theory and practice.

As the case was very complex and involved not only Jay, but other key individuals from his family and business, the coach also demonstrated good leadership skills and mediation.

Last but not least, the coach was sensitive to cultural differences. The role of the family was extremely important, so she actively involved key individuals in the coaching process and organised group sessions at the end to conclude the process.

The coach has also demonstrated the ability to match the coaching approach with the culture-specific preferences for more complex approach to business, where family and work was intertwined, values were shared and the two were not disconnected (Shams, 2006).

Continuing professional development and supervision: achieving competency and efficiency

The literature is indicating the value of assessing coaching performance to facilitate knowledge building exercises in coaching practice, and to develop appropriate coaching approaches, tools and techniques (Branbender, 2010). The best coaching practice is always driven by a coach's good understanding of the coaching needs, and competent use of relevant tools and techniques. In addition, coaching effectiveness depends on antecedent factors, such as motivation of a coach (Horn, 2002). Autonomous motivation is particularly relevant here because it refers to three major psychological needs—autonomy, competence, and relatedness (MacLean, Mallett & Newcomb, 2012). If coaching itself is a learning process then motivation plays a major role to gain the maximum learning benefits from the coaching sessions, including expected coaching outcomes. There is no research evidence on coaching motivation for family businesses. However, this issue is particularly important due to the special attention and motivation needed to manage sensitive and confidential family issues in a business context. MacLean and colleagues (2012) warned against the use of "one size fits all" notion of any coaching approach, and argued for more research to understand the underlying motivation of coaching behaviour to assess effective coaching intervention.

Supervision is an important part of continuing professional development and the following case study is demonstrating the value of supervision in a coaching practice. Peer and normal supervision (normal supervision is referring to supervision with a senior coach or coaching psychologist, and one-to-one sessions) is the most important CPD activity to provide quality assurance, learning and development for the coach practitioner, and assures that the coachees are getting the best service possible. Even though supervision is not an obligatory activity we would strongly recommend that this is in place regardless of the stage the coach is in. Supervision sessions enable the coach to reflect on the cases, investigate various intervention options and discuss any professional and personal issues. The following case study is demonstrating the role of supervision in coaching.

Case study 3: supervision

The coach has addressed this difficult case. Susan leads a property management business with her extended family. She has a history of mental health issues, including eating disorders and depression.

Her main reason for coming to the coach was to work on her leadership skills. Due to the history of her mental health she feels that other family members that work in family business do not really see her as the business leader. However, she feels that they follow her lead, not because they would respect her leadership skills, but because they feel sorry for her. She is also quite anxious not to fall back into eating disorders and depression. She is on medication and has received psychotherapy and she feels that this will not interfere with her coaching process working on her leadership skills.

In the first session, the coach clarified the differences between coaching and psychotherapy and clearly explained her limitations in the process.

By doing that the coach explained the domain of coaching and the purpose of the coaching process—which was in this case developing leadership skills. The coach also explained her competencies and made clear that she is not trained to deal with mental health issues. The client and the coach agreed should any of the mental health problems flair up, Susan would be seeking extra help from her psychotherapist.

The coach, therefore, made sure that the safety net was put in place. However, the coach was still unsure about whether she was competent enough to continue with the case, so she decided to use one of her supervision sessions to discuss the issues. The major areas of the dialogues between a coach and her supervisor are presented below to demonstrate the dynamics of the supervision:

Coach: I am really concerned that there may be other underlying issues with the client and that leadership skills are just something on the surface.

Supervisor: What makes you think that leadership skills are a surface issue?

Coach: Well, she suffered from an eating disorder and depression. I felt that the client was struggling with control issues and my concern is that if she goes too far out of her comfort zone in the coaching process, she will feel too much out of control and she will fall back to eating/depression.

Supervisor: These concerns are justified. However, you clarified with her what the coaching process was, what you will focus on and what your competencies are. Why do you think you are still concerned about it?

Coach: I am not sure. Perhaps I am not confident enough in my skills ... Maybe I am afraid that things will go out of control.

Supervisor: It is good that you are thinking about it. Have you put any safety measures in place if that happens?

Coach: Yes, we discussed that, so there are things in place.

Supervisor: It seems that you have taken the required steps to protect both the client and yourself.

Coach: Yes, I think I have. However, as I have never dealt with someone who had a serious eating disorder, so I feel a bit unsure about everything.

Supervisor: This is completely understandable. It seems, however, that you are aware of your own competencies and limitations.

Coach: Yes, I am. In that case I think I can handle the situation, as we will focus on leadership issues and perhaps on her self-confidence as well.

Supervisor: It seems that you have a good coaching plan, that both you and the coachee agree on … coach: Yes, we do.

Supervisor: Is there anything else that you can do to improve your practice in this case?

Coach: I will look up any research on coaching people with mental health problems. Maybe I can also ask if any other coachee in my peer group has any experience with this. If I do that that will make me feel much more confident to deal with this case.

The coach kept working with Susan and her family. It became apparent that her family appreciated her leadership skills and they were not following her lead because of her mental health history. A couple of group coaching sessions at the end helped the team to become more coherent. Susan was comfortable to show her insecurities to other family/business members, without the fear of losing her leadership credentials.

Learning from the case study

- The coach has to be aware of their own skills and competencies.
- The importance of supervision and reflection.
- Coaching and counselling sometimes overlap in family businesses and is therefore crucial that the coach is aware of their limitations.
- Coaching contract with the client is crucial in a difficult case.
- The coach exhibits good professional practice.

The coach was unsure about this complex case. She was particularly weary of her client's mental health issues that could interfere or surface during coaching. The coach brought this out at a couple of supervision sessions. The supervisor guided the coach to reflect on her decision-making process, agreed on coaching plan with the clients and her own competencies. The reflection is useful also to link the decisions with research evidence and the evidence from her own practice. As the supervisor asks the questions, the coach evaluates her own decisions and her own work. She voices some of her insecurities. The supervisor then guides the coach to take further steps to learn more about this specific motivation. The coach shows high motivation to do so—which will make the learning process more effective. The coach shows that she follows a specific code of practice and is aware of generic and specific competencies.

The supervision sessions provide the space for reflection, but also show the elements of coaching. The supervisor encourages the coach to explore different options to deal with the problem and guides the coach to additional learning from published evidence-based theory and practice, and peer practitioners.

The key learning elements from supervision is presented in Table 8.2.

Table 8.2 Major learning elements from supervision in a coaching context

Ability to assess your own competencies	For example, using performance-related evaluation questionnaire, reflective diary for coaching sessions, coachees' feedback.
Case formulations	Using a set case formulation plan that is discussed in peer or regular supervision. The case formulation will provide the coach with a set of intervention hypotheses the will direct and justify the coaching intervention.
Clearly set boundaries of coaching intervention	Using a coaching contract explain to the client where the boundaries and competencies are.
Reflective practitioner	The use of reflective diary, supervision and client feedback helps to examine your own practice.
Learning about new issues and acknowledging limitations	The above will clarify necessary learning points and required CPD activities.
Following the relevant code of practice	In the above case the coach follows the BPS (British Psychological Society) and the ISCP (International Society for Coaching Psychology) Code of Practice. Membership in a reputable professional organisation provides support and practice guidelines to protect the client and the practitioner.

Critical issues in assessing performance

The literature on coaching efficacy is dominated by Horn's model of coaching efficacy (2002) as it has provided a robust approach to understand coaching efficacy in the context of a coach's behaviour. The model has proposed three key factors affecting a coach's behaviour, antecedent factors which include both a coachee and a coach's personal characteristics, and organisational context, second, a coach's behaviour and expectation affecting the coachee's performance and evaluation of the coaching intervention and third, situational factors such as emotional responses, vulnerability of the coachee, and individual differences in coaching style and behaviour.

Coaching efficacy is defined as a coach's perceived beliefs and understanding about his/her capability to affect the behaviour of the coachee in a coaching context (Feltz, Chase, Moritz & Sullivan, 1999). Coaching efficacy is also the single most strong predictor of the effectiveness of coaching behaviour (Myers, Wolf & Feltz, 2005). A coaching efficacy tool can guide a coach to assess his/her "fitness for coaching", and the coaching efficacy scale by Feltz and colleagues (1999) is serving this purpose. However, more research is needed to develop tools and techniques using appropriate approaches for assessing a family business coach's performance-related behaviour. Another issue in this context is also to identify any special measures and assessments needed for facilitating ethical and effective coaching intervention for family businesses. This is particularly important as family businesses require sensitive and family-focused approach in coaching, and a coach must exhibit appropriate behaviour to satisfy family-focused coaching in a business context. A coach's behaviour needs to be monitored and evaluated appropriately to meet professional standards and ethical requirements in a family business context, but this issue is still to be subjected to any professional regulation in the UK. However, the call for benchmarking coaching skills and to professionalise coaching practice is demonstrating the importance of assessing a coach's behaviour in a coaching context (Grant, Passmore, Cavanagh & Parker, 2010). Pelz-Linder (2014) has used an action research approach to justify the value of research on benchmarking coaching skills as it involves coaching practitioners' direct involvement to provide evidence, and to inform their own practice. We can apply this approach in assessing a family business coach's performance and a reflective learning approach may also add further value to develop good and ethical coaching practice.

The major critical issues in assessing coaching performance are summarised below:

- Alignment of family dynamics to business issues.
- Professional scrutiny of coaching practices and standard of delivery using existing ethical requirements and professional standards.
- Coachee-focused approaches and promoting non-judgemental and fair approaches to coach diverse groups with appropriate consideration of equality and diversity policy.
- Appropriate attention to power balance between a coach and a coachee, respecting confidentiality.
- Critical combination of generic and specific competencies.
- Self-evaluation of coaching skills and competencies via self-assessment (core values, CPD), supervision and feedback from coaches.

Conclusion

The success of any coaching intervention depends on the competent and efficacious performance of a coach. Good coaching practices can be ensured if practitioners' performance is monitored and regulated by a set of formal standards, similar to good academic practices set out by the higher education academy, UK. It is important to explore how performance-related assessments could guide us to detect specific competencies required for the delivery of effective coaching interventions. This can be achieved using selected tools and techniques for self-assessments, and existing practices, such as peer coaching and supervision. Family businesses require value-based coaching approaches, which should be reflected in the set of skills and competencies of the coach focusing on the business practice. Using real-life case studies and authors' knowledge-depth, the critical discussion in this chapter is highlighting the need for performance-related assessments and reflection of competencies in performance. These are expected to benefit personal and professional development of a family business coach with a focus on learning from the coaching experiences on an on-going basis. The chapter has drawn attention to practitioners to consider coaching practice-related experiences as useful learning experiences and to use the learning for their personal and professional development.

References

Akpan, J. I., Udoh, P. A. E., & Adibisi, B. (2020). Small business awareness and adoption of state-of-the-art technologies in emerging and developing markets, and lessons from the COVID-19 pandemic. *Journal of Small Business and Entrepreneurship (online)* (accessed 8 February 2021).

Branbender, M. V. (2010). Book, software and test review section, editorial note. *Measurement in Physical Education and Exercise Science, 9*: 135–160.

Chelladurai, P. (1978). *A Contingency Model of Leadership in Athletics. Unpublished Doctoral Dissertation*, Ontario: University of Waterloo.

Feltz, D. L., Chase, M. A., Moritz, S. E., & Sullivan, P. J. (1999). A conceptual model of coaching efficacy: Preliminary investigation and instrument development. *Journal of Educational Psychology, 91*: 765–776.

Fransella, F., Bell, R., & Bannister, D. (2004). *A Manual for Repertory Grid Technique. Second Edition*. Chichester: John Wiley & Sons.

Grant, A. M., Passmore, J., Cavanagh, M. J., & Parker, H. (2010). The state of play in coaching today: A review of the field. *International Review of Industrial and Organisational Psychology, 25*: 125–167.

Horn, T. S. (2002). Coaching effectiveness in the sport domain. In: T. S. Horn (Ed.), *Advances in Sport Psychology* (2nd ed.) (pp. 309–354). Champaign, IL: Human Kinetics.

Horn, T. S. (2008). Coaching effectiveness in the sport domain. In: T. S. Horn (Ed.), *Advances in Sport Psychology* (pp. 239–267). Champaign, IL: Human Kinetics.

Kelly, G. A. (1955). *The Psychology of Personal Constructs*. New York, NY: Norton.

MacLean, N. K., Mallett, J. C., & Newcomb, P. (2012). Assessing coach motivation. The development of the coach motivation questionnaire (CMQ). *Journal of Sport & Exercise Psychology, 34*: 184–207.

Mattioli, D. (2009). Recession spells end for many family business. *Wall Street Journal*. 6 October 2009, p. B6. Retrieved from http://online.wsj.com/article/SB12547839942 9765967.html. Last accessed 30 April 2011.

Myers, D. N., Wolfe, W. E., & Feltz, L. D. (2005). An evaluation of the psychometric properties of the coaching efficacy scale for coaches from the United States of America. *Measurement in Physical Education and Exercise Science, 9*: 135–160.

Pelz-Linder, S. (2014). Steps towards the benchmarking of coaches' skills. *International Journal of Evidence Based Coaching and Mentoring, 12*(1): 47–62.

Shams, M. (2006). Approaches in business coaching: Exploring context-specific and cultural issues. In: M. Shams & P. Jackson (Eds.), *Developments in Work and Organizational Psychology* (pp. 229–244). The Netherlands: Elsevier/Emerald.

Shams, M. (2011). Key issues in family business coaching. In: M. Shams & D. Lane (Eds.), *Coaching in the Family Owned Business: A Path to Growth* (pp. 1–12). London/New York: Routledge.

Sullivan, P., Paquette, J. K., Holt, L. N., & Bloom, A. J. (2012). The relation of coaching context and coach education to coaching efficacy and perceived leadership behaviors in youth sport. *The Sport Psychologist, 26*: 122–134.

Walach-Bista, Z. (2013). A polish adaptation of leadership scale for sports: A questionnaire examining coaching behaviour. *Human Development, 14*: 265–274.

Appendix 8.1

An example of the application of repertory grid technique is presented below:
  A completed Repertory Grid: an example

A modified Repertory Grid was used with a small family business producing and trading with high-end luxury furniture. The business was led by Simon and his wife Nina. They both covered different parts of the business.

The coach was called in as there were a lot of conflicts between staff, confusion over role divisions and Simon was unsure whether to continue with the business. After the case formulation, the coach decided to use REP grid (reference) as a method to increase Simon's awareness of his own values and how these overlap with the values of his organisation and staff.

Stage 1

The client was asked to come up with the names of his employees, including his family members that were involved in his business. He was asked to compare and contrast them in terms of their values, work commitment, personality traits, etc.

The descriptors the client produced were put in a grid. Simon was then asked to produce the opposite of each descriptor that he provided. Individual members of staff, including Simon and Nina were rated on the grid. All grids were then compared, which helped Simon to increase his awareness of how he perceived the value system in his organisation. The same exercise was done with other key members of staff and all family members involved in the business. The grids were compared.

Simon

Committed	1	2	3	4	5	Does not care
Good leader	1	2	3	4	5	Follower
Enthusiastic	1	2	3	4	5	Lazy
Empathic	1	2	3	4	5	Selfish

Learning outcomes

- Increased awareness of client's own core values.
- Increased awareness of core values of other key members of staff (including all family members involved in business).
- More clarity on organisational values.
- Restructuring and clarity of roles.
- Some family members, whose values were not coherent and were not very engaged in the business decided not to get involved in strategic planning of the organisation.

Chapter 9

Team coaching in family business

Manfusa Shams

Introduction

Team coaching can provide the means to optimise collective talent. Team coaching explores issues related to individuals in a team as well as a team collectively, as such, team coaching is the most effective intervention for improving family functions and their business functions. Family Business Team coaching is different from traditional team coaching because the focus is on the family team as a single business unit to foster team performance and improving family relationships to impact on business sustainability.

Typically, a family business coaching involves leadership coaching and executive coaching, different psychodynamic approaches, family therapy, etc.

A family business represents a business team and all activities are built around a family business rather than for a family. It is a business for the wide society by the family members as a business team. Hence, it is important to explore team coaching in a family business context.

This chapter aims to present critical reflective analysis of team coaching effectiveness to achieve the expected coaching outcomes, and the learning embedded in the practice to design and deliver appropriate team coaching for a family business. An interdisciplinary approach is used to discuss critical issues in an effective team coaching. The need for team coaching intervention for a family business is highlighted using relevant examples.

> ### Key questions
> - What is team coaching in a family business context?
> - How is team coaching different to group coaching?
> - How team coaching can minimise the risk of business failure?
> - What are the success factors in team coaching?
> - What are the learning issues inherent in team coaching for a practitioner to improve their practice?

DOI: 10.4324/9781003174721-9

A family business represents a group/team in business with family members, hence, team coaching is the most appropriate approach to support sustainable team development (Shams & Lane, 2020). Team coaching aims to strengthen individuals with a focus on building a strong functional team (Britton, 2013). Team coaching is different from group coaching because of the emphasis on capacity building of a team, team effectiveness, team values, and shared behavioural norms (Britton, 2015). Group coaching is usually regarded as an extension of individual coaching, when an organisation needs to provide a safe conversational space for selected employees to explore and share critical issues affecting their performance and integration. Team coaching involves direct interaction with a team to support collective efforts to accomplish a business task using their collective resources (Hackman & Wageman, 2005). Team coaching is different from individual coaching because the focus is on the team as whole to foster team performance, and to facilitate collective team efforts to generate a common goal for the business growth.

Team coaching and group coaching from a family business context

A family business refers to a business owned by family members, which may or may not be founded by a family member (Shams, 2006).

Family business coaching is characterised by a blended approach in coaching in which a coaching intervention must incorporate family functionality issues along with business functions. There are growing concerns about which comes first—family or business (Shams, 2011). This leads to the critical question—if a team approach in family business can address both a family and their business simultaneously?

Team coaching can provide the means to optimise collective talent, and help to explore issues related to individuals in a team, as well as a team collectively. As such, team coaching is the most effective intervention for improving family functions in a family business context.

A group coaching approach refers to a group setting for the individual members to explore, discuss, share and evaluate their own issues affecting their performance and engagement with the family business, without divorcing the team's goal of achieving sustainable growth of their family business. The application of group coaching is diverse, for example, individual business owners with a shared goal of their own business improvement. This can also be applied to a group who may not be a team, for example, a parenting group (Britton, 2013). The challenges facing each individual and the shared understanding of the mechanisms to deal with the challenges in a group coaching session can provide peer support, mutual trust and collaborative learning. This approach, however, can be difficult to apply to a family business as it is regarded as a business team and not a social group with shared interests.

A team coaching approach is appropriate for a family business team as this approach can provide the opportunity to develop insights and multiple perspectives, stronger working relations, and collaborative learning. Maintaining individual presence distinctively in a team can benefit the team as a whole due to the rich level of engagement and participation in the discussion, in which individual views are encouraged, valued and appreciated.

The debate does not necessarily lead to a sharp distinction between the effectiveness of group vs. team coaching in a family business context. Rather, this may lead to the powerful argument in favour of an integrated approach for the family business, for example, applying both individual/group and team coaching at different stages of the coaching intervention.

Team coaching for a family business: an example

The Walkers are a close-knit family and set up family property business using their own skills and experiences. Despite drawing a business plan, investing their own funds and having the business model sorted, they were struggling to achieve their financial target with no growth in their business. A coach hired by the family identified that the family is running their business in terms status quo in the family, and the relationship issues and inter family communication were posing as threats to make any progress, including taking any risks to develop their business. The coach started with helping the family to understand the underlying causes of the risk of the business failure. These include reluctance to disagree with and/or offer constructive suggestions to other older members due to the fear of upsetting the other members. The coach highlighted that the family role has to be separated from the business role and *the family must work as a team* with equal opportunity to contribute to the family business. The coach worked with them to improve assertiveness and openness, and encouraged them to revisit business operation, decision making and risk analysis to include team efforts and collective input. The coach could also introduce Belbin's team role (2013) to help family members to understand, appreciate and accept different roles each member can take in relation to the business development. See Chapter 1 for further discussion on team role.

The case study here is demonstrating that a family business may not start as a family team in business (Shams & Lampshire, 2016). However, a family business is at the risk of failure if they do not work together as a team. A coach can provide the direction, guidance and support in this context.

A family is a single social unit hence, a family business can also be considered as a single business unit, which is operated by a team of family members (Shams, 2011). A closely linked discipline in this context is family coaching, which refers to the application of a strength-based approach to foster growth in family relations, and to facilitate family functions (Allen & Huff, 2014). A family coaching approach provides the family team a trusted platform to share their concerns, understand critical family issues and develop insights in their family functions. A team coaching intervention is valuable to assist the family to progressive development and growth (Borus et al., 2018). The focus in family coaching is enabling and maximising both individual and collective potentials of the family team. Family coaching approach can be aligned to family business coaching approach except that the business team coaching involves issues relating to the development and growth of a family business. Previously, I have debated on the two-tier coaching approach for a family business—one for the family as a team, and another for the family business as a functional business team (Shams, 2011). An effective coaching intervention for a family involves an integrated family and business coaching simultaneously (Shams & Lane, 2017).

Success factors in team coaching

Team coaching provides the unique opportunity to a family business to share and learn from each other which otherwise is not possible in a constraint business environment where the dominant issues are level of productivity and expected business profits. The positive outcomes from team coaching are involvement of each family member, gaining new knowledge, personal and professional skills enhancement, deep understanding of collective efforts for successful business functions, and collaborative ongoing learning through business operations (Vesso & Alas, 2016).

The success factors in team coaching are influenced by team characteristics, organisational strategies and objectives (Solansky & McIver, 2017). In addition, family dynamics is an important determinant of successful team coaching intervention. The team must be well structured with a good flow of communication, understanding, and supported by the leader to gain the positive coaching outcomes (Goldman et al., 2013). This precondition is difficult to achieve for a family business team due to the traditional hierarchical team structure and imbalance on power structure in business functions. Although, these factors are considered as strengths by many family businesses, however, these are not necessarily leading to sustained progressive business development (Peters & Carr, 2013).

Hence, it is important to offer coaching to a family team prior to a family business team in order to iron out any conflicts and constraints in business operation. A team coaching approach can offer a secured professional space for the personal and professional development of a coaching practitioner as well as for the family team (Solansky & McIver, 2017).

The role of a coach is another critical success factor. The dominant critical success factors, (1) coaching outcomes, (2) coachee readiness, (3) coach-team relationship, (4) coachee engagement, (5) sustained changes. Figure 9.1 represents the critical success factors in team coaching.

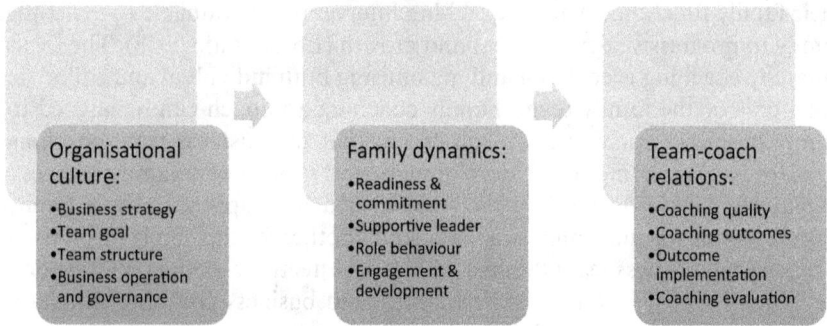

Figure 9.1 Success factors in team coaching.

The three major success factors (organisational culture, family dynamics, team-coach relations) are important in a family business context, particularly, family dynamics. This implies that family dynamics is central to achieve effective coaching intervention, and the success of this intervention will influence the coaching quality and the subsequent coaching outcome.

Based on the discussion above, four stages of family team coaching are identified:

Stage 1: Organisational culture—family business
Stage 2: Family dynamics in business
Stage 3: Coaching approach and coaching outcomes
Stage 4: Implementation and evaluation

For each stage, a coach can use a Likert-type scale both at the beginning (first step) and at the end of a coaching intervention (second step) to assess the effect of coaching interventions.

Stage 1: organisational culture in a family business

A family business context can indicate the prevailing organisational culture, particularly, if it is regulated by family traditions in which a senior family member leads the business management. The trend is much less common in recent years due to the exposure of modern technologies, and advance competency levels of younger generations in a family business. In many instances, a senior family member serves only as a nominal leader with majority of business management is carried out by skilled young family members.

The following scale is designed for the family business to support team coaching intervention both at the beginning and after the coaching intervention to identify the family business culture (first step), and the changes in family business culture after the coaching intervention (second step).

Organisational culture in a family business scale

Please rate your organisation from a structural perspective. The structural perspective refers to the family business team composition, task distribution, communication and transparency.

Very good	Good	Unsure	Not good	worse
1	2	3	4	5

Stage 2: family dynamics in business

A family business is built on family dynamic, hence, it is important to establish the family as a business team. Most of the time, a family business fails to separate critical family relationship issues from the business operation (Shams & Lane, 2020). A team coaching approach can provide the relevant tools and techniques for the family to develop a team approach in business irrespective of kinship and relational issues. However, the success of a team approach must accompany a checkpoint to ascertain the family dynamics. The family dynamics include family cohesion, integration and inclusion (Shams & Lampshire, 2016). The checkpoint below is an example which a coach can apply to each family member to address their family dynamics prior to the coaching intervention. There is no "one size fits all" checkpoint as family dynamics are varied and a checkpoint should accommodate this diversity.

A checkpoint for family dynamics

Please provide your response in relation to the family business and your role assignment.

1	Who is the founder?
2	How the business is operated (structure) = remote/technology aided/both/others (please specify)?
3	What is your assigned role?
4	How long are you involved in this family business?
5	How is your communication with the founder and others in business?
6	How would you rate your performance and what would you like to achieve at present and in the future?

Stage 3: coaching approach and coaching outcomes

Team coaching can bring increasing positive outcomes for a family business team. With this vision, a coach needs to finalise the approach for intervention. This can be accomplished using the following questions:

- What will get priority—team coaching/family coaching?
- How this will be delivered and how the intervention will affect the coaching outcome?

Stage 4: implementation and evaluation

The success factors in team coaching are driving forces to bring a change in family business operation towards sustainable progress. Any change can be evident through the implementation of the coaching outcomes and evaluation afterwards.

A coach needs to formulate a plan for delivering the coaching outcome for implementation. An example of this plan is provided below.

Coaching outcome delivery and implementation plan

Coaching outcome delivery can be offered in a family team setting to ensure that response from each family member is considered, and further dialogues from a family team is incorporated in the coaching implementation plan as set out below.

Coaching outcome implementation plan

> Step 1: Which part of the outcome will be implemented first?
> Step 2: Who will be involved in the implementation?
> Step 3: How the coaching implementation outcome will be evaluated?
> Step 4: When the changes caused by the implementation can be assessed?
> Step 5: How a team approach to implement the coaching outcome will be applied?
> Step 6: To what extent a coach can provide support for implementation?
> Step 7: How the family team engagement can be assured during implementation?

Engaging a family team in the implementation and evaluation of coaching outcome is likely to empower the team to make continuous progress in their personal and professional development, as well as their family business.

The implementation outcomes in family team coaching are:

- Enhanced performance with collaborative effort to reach peak performance as a team.
- Enabling and maximising individual member's input.
- Opening potential pathway to success through exploration, planning and development of critical issues affecting their family business.

- Improved family functioning both beyond and within a family business.

Team coaching provides the platform for a family to learn and share issues affecting their personal as well as business development. It thus contains participation and acquisition metaphor in learning (Shams, 2013; Shams and Lane, 2018). A family team can acquire knowledge and understanding from the coaching process. Their full participation and engagement in all discussions and critical appraisal of their performance in business functions both at an individual and team basis can help to achieve the maximum benefits from the coaching interventions.

Learning issues for a practitioner

A coaching practice is likely to benefit both the practitioners and the recipients. It is a reciprocal learning process in which a practitioner learns from the delivery of the coaching intervention and the recipients obtain the benefits from the coaching engagement and implementation.

The reflective learning practitioner in a coaching context is in a privileged position to negotiate ongoing learning from the practice with the existing practice-related approach. The opportunity to involve with the developmental part of a family business brings new knowledge, understanding of, and insights in the coaching practice. Hence, the coaching practitioner is also professionally developing along with the coachee. Grant (2011) has highlighted the value of learning from each coaching sessions and the learning is emerged from a process of reviewing and evaluating each coaching sessions.

If the learning from the team coaching sessions can be aligned with the coaching delivery approach and outcome evaluation process, then team coaching is expected to bring equal level of benefits for both the coach and the coachee (Shams, 2016).

In a team coaching context, the learning embedded in coaching sessions through this feedback loop can be used to design subsequent sessions according to coaching needs for individual family members in business. This approach thus provides depth in learning from the coaching practice. Figure 9.2 is depicting the impact of feedback loop on the learning process for both the practitioners and the coachee.

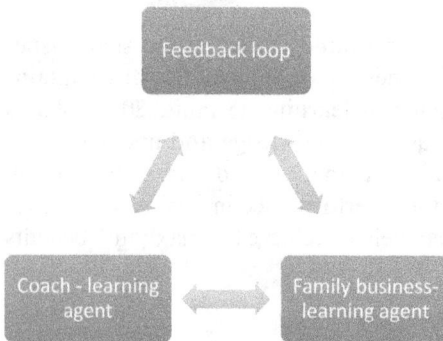

Figure 9.2 Feedback loop in team coaching.

Conclusion

Team coaching is an important coaching approach. It is frequently used in various organisations. However, the use of team coaching in a family business context is not researched and documented appropriately. The deconstruction of the popular assumption of a family business as "family matter" or "family issues in a business" necessitates the application of a team coaching approach to value and recognise a family business as a business team. The changing and wide acceptance of family business as an important business organisation demands a progressive move for the family business team to a professional business team.

However, it is difficult to consider a family business as a business team similar to any non-family business because of the family ties and generational issues. Hence, team coaching may need to be delivered to a family team and for a family business team either simultaneously or separately to identify critical family issues affecting a family in business, and critical business issues affecting a family business team.

In this chapter, I have highlighted the importance of team coaching for a family business, the success factors and learning from family business team coaching. The chapter has also provided four stages of team coaching with a set of guidance for the practitioners to consider for application to their coaching practice.

A family business will benefit from a team coaching approach if they value a team approach in their business and make an effort to separate out family relations issues from their family business functions. Team coaching can provide the rich platform for a family to thrive both at the personal and business levels. Team coaching for a family business can help us to understand the significant contribution of coaching practice to a family business using a team lens. Team coaching is a universal concept and a generic approach which can be applied to any business irrespective of contextual factors, differential business operations, business visions and goals.

This discussion in this chapter is confirming the powerful impact of team coaching on the sustained development of a family business.

References

Allen, K., & Huff, N. (2014). Family coaching: An emerging family science field. *Family Relations, 63*(5), 569–582.

Britton, J. (2013). *From One to Many: Best Practices for Team and Group Coaching.* Toronto: Jossey-Bass.

Britton, J. J. (2015). Expanding the coaching conversation: group and team coaching. *Industrial and Commercial Training, 47*(3), 116–120.

Belbin, R. (2013). *Management Teams: Why They Succeed or Fail?* London: Routledge.

Borus, R., Jane, M., Dallas, S., Erin, S., & Maryann, K. (2018). Family coaching as a delivery modality for evidence-based prevention programs. *Clinical Child Psychology and Psychiatry, 23*(1): 96–109.

Goldman, E., Wesner, M. & Karnchanomai, O. (2013). Reciprocal peer coaching: A critical contributor to implementing individual leadership plans. *Human Resource Development Quarterly, 24*(1): 63–87.

Grant, A. (2011). Is it time to REGROW the GROW model? *Issues Related to Teaching Coaching Session Structures, 7*(2): 118–127.

Hackman, J. R., & Wageman, R. (2005). A theory of team coaching. *Academy of Management Review, 30*(2), 269–287.

Peters, J. & Carr, C. (2013). Team effectiveness and team coaching literature review. *Coaching: An International Journal of Theory, Research and Practice, 6*(2): 116–136.

Shams, M. (2006). Approaches in Business Coaching; exploring context-specific and cultural issues. In M. Shams & P. Jackson (Eds.), *Developments in Work and Organizational Psychology* (pp. 229–244). Oxford: Elsevier.

Shams, M. (2011). Key issues in family business coaching. In Shams, M. & Lane, D. (Eds.), *Coaching in the family owned business: a path to growth* (pp. 1–12). London: Karnac.

Shams, M. (2013) Communities of coaching practice: Developing a new approach. *International Coaching Psychology Review, 8*(2): 89–91.

Shams, M. (2016). Learning from family business coaching practices. In M. Shams and D Lane (Eds.), *Supporting the Family Business: A Coaching Practitioner's Handbook* (pp. 1–14). London: Routledge.

Shams, M. & Lampshire, J. (2016). Group dynamics in coaching family business: A focused, integrated and inclusive approach. In M. Shams and D. Lane (Eds.) *Supporting the Family Business: A Coaching Practitioner's Handbook* (pp. 43–66). London: Routledge.

Shams, M., & Lane, D. (2017). Blended coaching for family business. *Coaching at Work, 12*(1): 41–43.

Shams, M., & Lane, D. (2018). Family relations: Coaching techniques for a family business. *The Coaching Psychologist, 14*(1): 34–41.

Shams, M., & Lane, D. (2020). Team coaching and family business. *The Coaching Psychologist, 16*(1): 25–33.

Solansky, S., & McIver, D. (2017). Team characteristics and leadership training participation. *Team Performance Management, 24*(3/4): 135–149.

Vesso, S., & Alas, R. (2016). Characteristics of a coaching culture in leadership style the leader's impact on culture. *Problems and Perspectives in Management, 14*(2): 306–318.

Chapter 10

Future directions and conclusions

Manfusa Shams

Introduction

Coaching psychology is developing fast as a practice-based discipline; hence, attention needs to be paid to the professional development and personal learning of practitioners in a coaching context (Shams, 2013). One of the significant areas of development is the delivery of discipline-focused coaching approach, tools and techniques. Family business coaching is one such area in which a focused approach is needed to provide a robust coaching intervention for the benefits of a family business because the intervention requires a blended approach in which equal attention must be paid to a family and a business (Shams, 2011).

With the increasing high percentage of contributions from the family businesses to the national economy all over the world (Whatley, 2011), it is important to focus attention to coaching practitioners who are engaged in family business coaching. This is because the coaching practices are dealing with the complex interface between a family and their businesses. The contributions of related disciplines are immense in family business coaching, and both interdisciplinary and multidisciplinary techniques are in frequent use in coaching practice without any explicit reference to this practice.

A new frontier of family business: environmental challenge

The economic growth is sterile at present because of the restricted social and economic mobility caused by the COVID-19 pandemic. However, family businesses are playing a major role to reverse this trend as the failing industry employees are increasingly moving towards a family businesses pathway as an alternative to paid employment, which can also ensure economic security in a major crisis.

The economic performance in a society is determined by a multitude of factors. The complex interdependencies suggest that the domino effect of COVID-19 pandemic has brought a major challenge for family businesses.

DOI: 10.4324/9781003174721-10

For example, a family business needs to rely on the major manufacturing industries for operational purposes and if these are economically declining then that will have an impact on a family business performance. These challenging issues are important for a coach to include to address the coaching needs of a family business.

A family business is continuing to be the major economic driving force irrespective of any natural disaster and pandemic effect as this trend is evident over the years. Hence the question is if we can expect any change of this trend in this pandemic due to the new way of working in which family members have to embrace new technologies to sustain the pressure from the increasing risk for failure. In addition, knowledge and understanding of the manufacturing process and delivery of goods will require new rules and regulations, and shipments cautionary measures. This new way of performing business can be stressful to a family business as this requires advance training and coordinated teamwork. Personal health and safety issues need to be prioritised to adhere to the lockdown restrictions, social distancing and restricted mobility options.

However, a few research has highlighted the positive consequences of this pandemic and this relates to the growing interests to implement advance cutting-edge technology in business operations and delivery, and gaining relevant experiences to achieve competitive advantage (Akpan et al., 2020). A family business coach thus requires to consider these advance changing nature of a family business in their coaching approach.

Family business coaching can provide a strong arm for the family business to consider it as an effective coping strategy and a crisis management tool (Ratten, 2020). The merge of this new way of family business and other business functions will bring a new trend in the working practice, and may minimise the differences between these two economic sectors with an expectation of increasing mutual partnership and economic collaboration. Family businesses as such can provide a strong motivational agent to inspire failing economy to recover using this alternative economic pathway. A coaching practitioner is in a privilege position to help the failing business sectors towards a viable economic option using a family business coaching model as a good example for economic recovery.

Coaching practice itself is a learning and professional development activity. We have argued for extrapolating major learning areas from a coaching practice in a family business context. Taking family business coaching as a learning object, we have identified key areas of learning from the coaching practice for a practitioner. These areas are coaching as a learning process (Chapter 1), practice-related learning (Chapter 2), delivering family business coaching using a family-centred approach (Chapter 3), learning from the interaction between families and their businesses (Chapter 4), natural emergence of learning from coaching practices, referred to as "auto-learning" (Chapter 5), learning from the coaching outcomes (Chapter 6), learning from the application of interdisciplinary approaches (Chapter 7), learning from coaching practices with a focus on coaching practitioner's performance-related learning and assessments (Chapter 8) and team coaching for a family business (Chapter 9).

The main theme running through all chapters is "learning from different parts of a coaching intervention" from a family business perspective. Taking a bird's-eye view, we have extrapolated essential learning issues from selected case studies and coaching experiences, with an aim to facilitate the coaching practitioners' personal and professional development. Our focus was on generating knowledge-base and interests in further research to support good family business coaching practice.

The summary of discussions in each chapter is presented below to highlight the emerging learning issues from coaching practices.

Emerging issues

Informal learning from coaching

We have argued that the learning from coaching practices is informal learning (Chapter 1) and needs to be structured, formalised and shared to assess the value of this learning in practice. This informal learning can be a good source to add to further knowledge and understanding of practice-related issues. The ability to extrapolate and identify learning from the coaching practice is likely to enhance growth in practice, and can provide sustained outcomes. It also has an economic benefit, for example, "auto-learning" from the coaching intervention can be a powerful learning tool without any extra cost to obtain training in this area. The authentification of this learning can be achieved from the successful and sustained coaching outcomes. We have presented evidence-based discussion in Chapter 5 about this issue. However, systematic research to assess the value of learning from the coaching practice for the coach, and professional initiatives to document the learning should be carried out, with a focus to develop the practical application of coaching psychology.

Learning curve

A coach can learn on a continuous basis from the coaching practice but a learning curve can help to detect the progression in learning, as well as to identify the practitioners' developmental needs. As such a learning timeline needs to be drawn at the beginning of a coaching intervention to identify the critical learning points from "in-coaching" and "end coaching" parts of coaching timeline (please see Chapter 1 for further discussion). This can be done using our suggested tools and techniques in all chapters, and using recording facility of all sessions, as well as peer-coaching. This approach will help to structure the learning and for verification purposes.

The challenging issue is what approach can help to achieve the maximum learning benefits from the coaching practice—a coachee-focused or a coach-focused approach? Although, the existing practices are predominantly using a coachee-focused approach to serve the needs of the coachees, however, a coach can get useful learning experience if they apply a coach-focused coaching intervention. This issue can be resolved using an integrated and blended approach in which both the coach and the coachee can learn simultaneously, as such this is a task for the coach to manage using appropriate approaches, tools and techniques. We have provided relevant tools, techniques and tips in all chapters, and we hope coaching practitioners will find them useful and apply to their own practices.

Alignment of family with business in coaching practices

Family business coaching is characterised by coaching for the family and their business. Our critical discussion in Chapter 2 has demonstrated the importance of understanding the interdependency between families and their businesses. We have offered a few relevant activities for the coach to develop skills in this area. The alignment of family with their business in a coaching practice can ensure maximum benefits from the coaching intervention, and it is important for a coach to demonstrate this in their practice. We have provided useful tips about this in Chapter 4, and our discussion was justified and supported by relevant real-life case studies.

LaManna (2013) has argued for the operation of two systems in a family business—family systems which is guided by emotional bond of family members and maintained by internal values, loyalty and protection, the other system is task-based and called "business system". This system operates by the competency and productivity of members. We have argued in Chapter 4 about the importance of alignment between family system and business system to deliver effective coaching interventions. There is evidence that dysfunctional families are contributing to business failure (LaManna, 2013), however, alignment of family to business functions is still not researched extensively. To highlight the importance of alignment issue, we have also offered relevant activities for the coaching practitioners to use in their own practices in Chapter 4.

Learning embedded in coaching practice

One of the major emerging issues from the discussions in all chapters is the implicit learning resources in coaching practices. Coaching practitioners can be benefitted with the learning experiences from their coaching practices, and the learning can thus provide a rich source of knowledge and understanding, albeit cognitive development of the coach. A coach can trace the learning components from all areas of coaching, however, we have selected a few major areas of coaching with significance of potential learning. These areas are natural learning from coaching, learning from coaching outcomes, learning from the interaction with the coachee, learning from the application of interdisciplinary approaches, tools and techniques, learning from the interdependency between families and their businesses. In Chapter 6, we have argued for the application of learning from the coaching outcomes and the need to integrate the learning in the practice. We have also provided key developmental issues from coaching outcomes and a few selected activities to extrapolate essential learning from the coaching outcomes. The collective learning experience is expected to provide rich learning resources for the coaching practitioners to develop, enhance and facilitate their coaching skills and professional development.

Coaching skills from the learning

Learning from coaching experiences can be used to develop relevant skills, techniques and tools. The process follows Kolb's learning cycle, in which reflection plays a major role to develop relevant coaching skills from on-going coaching practices and/coaching experiences. Chapter 6 offers a few relevant activities and assessments to map out the skills from the learning during the coaching sessions as well as at the end of the coaching sessions. These are referred to as learning skills from "in-coaching" and "end-coaching" stages of a coaching intervention. A coach is expected to develop relevant skills, tools and techniques from the learning in all areas of coaching practices, as such, our discussion in each chapter is enriched with relevant activities and assessments for the coach to develop insights and draw relevant tools and techniques to facilitate their practices. We have also demonstrated the way a coach can trace critical learning stages on a coaching timeline in Chapters 5 and 6.

Family-friendly and family-focused approach

The success of a family business depends on the effective design of an intervention and this can be achieved using a family-friendly and family-focused approach. A critical analysis on this issue is presented in Chapter 3. In Chapter 2, we have discussed the critical emotional connection between family members, and the role a coach can play to deal with complex family issues affecting their business. The case studies also have supported the arguments of managing family members' tensions arising from coaching sessions, and the need for a coach to develop professional skills to deal with complex family issues in a business context. The extent of knowledge about family dynamics needs to be assessed to ensure ethical and high professional performance in the delivery of family business coaching and this is critically discussed in Chapter 8.

Professional development and competency in practice

The overview of all chapters is indicating the need for a coach to develop their professional knowledge and understanding, relevant skills and practice-related competencies. The needs can be addressed using the learning from the coaching practitioner's practice. The general and specific competencies for delivering effective family business coaching are presented in Chapter 8.

Coaching is effective when a coach is able not only to bring successful outcomes but also to use the learning from the coaching for their professional development. However, without any formal way of assessing the learning from the coaching practices, it will not be possible to demonstrate the learning embedded in a practice, as such the activities and assessment in Chapter 8 are specially designed to apply to performance-related assessment, and to consider these as professional developmental activities.

Coaching for the family business team

A family business is characterised by a team of family members engaged in a business, hence, a team coaching approach can address complex functional issues in a family business, and provide appropriate support for the family business to grow as a business team. The new Chapter 9 has provided thoughtful discussions on the effectiveness of a team coaching approach, and the powerful role a family team can play to make sustainable business progress using an exclusive business team approach. Chapter 9 has provided a few professional development activities for the practitioners, and discussed the potential impact of a team coaching approach on mitigating a major environmental crisis.

Future directions: research and practice

We have provided critical analyses and thoughtful ideas of major learning issues in family business coaching practice with the aim to generate interests and research in this area. A good practice is always informed by relevant evidence and application of appropriate theories/models and framework. Our proposed activities and assessments will provide the groundwork to develop coaching practices in the context of family business. These may also serve as preliminary work to develop further practice-related approaches, tools and techniques by the coaching practitioners.

Coaching psychology is developing fast; however, the value of learning from the coaching practice is still not yet recognised widely. The popular coaching and mentoring service is unrelated to coaching psychological practice, yet the former service is very popular and obtaining state-funded initiative to apply the service to benefit the sport sector (North, 2010). Our aim in this book is to draw attention to policymakers, specialists, academics, practitioners and society in large to understand the immense value of coaching to help and improve family functions to develop and facilitate sustained family businesses. We are calling for more research, discussions and professional movement to establish the scientific status of coaching psychology practice and to popularise the application using a pragmatic professional developmental approach, with a focus on increasing learning from the coaching practices. We are expecting that our critical thoughtful analyses will generate interests in developing research- and practice-related knowledge and understanding, and also help to formalise the learning from coaching practices to facilitate the coaching practitioner's professional development and personal skill enhancement.

Conclusions

All learning arising from the coaching practices must be documented appropriately using relevant approaches, tools and techniques. This could be achieved from systematic research, publications, electronic and social media, collaborative and peer learning, and other formal modes such as conferences, workshops, training programmes and so on.

There are plenty of fragmented ideas about the value of coaching practices to enhance professional development, and we have tried to consolidate ideas to offer coherent discussions on coaching practice itself as a learning object. We have selected a few major learning areas from family business coaching practices. Our selection was based on our authors' skills and experiences, knowledge and understanding, as well as interests in developing these areas for their own practices.

Coaching practitioners must have the motivation to learn from their own practices, and share the learning with others to develop the practical application of coaching psychology. Also, identifying significant learning areas from the practices can facilitate further coaching practices, and this "auto-learning" may serve as an important impetus to personal development and growth in coaching practices, as well as professional insights in promoting coaching psychology as an applied discipline. The drive to apply the learning from practice can also ensure effective delivery as the coach will invest a carefully planned and designed intervention for achieving the learning outcomes. A systematic approach to trace learning elements from a coaching practice is needed, and the activities and assessments in all chapters are expected to provide useful resources to the practitioners' personal and professional development.

A diagram is presented below to present the learning areas from the selected parts of a coaching practice in this book.

Selected learning elements from different areas of coaching practices:

↓

- Auto-learning
- Learning from interaction

- Practice-related learning
- Learning from coaching outcomes
- Learning from family and business alignment
- Performance-related knowledge
- Experiential and reflective learning.

A coach can seek to explore one learning element at a time or all at once subject to their learning and developmental needs, nature and length of coaching intervention and accessibility to deliver a coach-focused coaching intervention. Our efforts to identify selected learning elements from the coaching practices are not limited to the above areas, rather they are starting areas of exploration to identify their benefits as well as scope for application to a coaching practice. I hope the critical and evidence-based discussions in this book by the practitioners will provide the groundwork for the coaching practitioners to appreciate the learning embedded in a coaching practice, and to apply the learning for their own personal and professional development. The arguments presented in this book will generate research and professional initiatives to value and recognise the significant contributions of family business coaching to develop coaching practices.

The book is enriched by the contributions from leading coaching practitioners and this first-hand coaching experience is a unique feature of this book, giving the opportunity to the readers to understand and learn challenging learning issues in coaching practices from a coaching practitioner's perspective.

References

Akpan, J. I., Udoh, P. A. E., & Adibisi, B. (2020). Small business awareness and adoption of state-of-the-art technologies in emerging and developing markets, and lessons from the COVID-19 pandemic Journal of small business and Entrepreneurship (online). https://doi.org/10.1080/08276331.2020.1820185 (accessed 8 February 2021).

LaManna, R. (2013). The two systems that make (or break) a family business. In *The Bottom Line* (pp. 42–43). USA: Rodman Publishing.

North, J. (2010). Using "coach developers" to facilitate coach learning and development: Qualitative evidence from the UK. *International Journal of Sports Science & Coaching, 5*: 239–256.

Ratten, V. (2020). Coronavirus (COVID-19) and entrepreneurship: Changing life and work landscape. *Journal of Small Business & Entrepreneurship, 32*(5): 503–516.

Shams, M. (2011). Key issues in family business coaching. In M. Shams & D. Lane (Eds.), *Coaching in the Family Owned Business: A Path to Growth* (pp. 1–12). London/New York: Routledge.

Shams, M. (2013). Communities of coaching practice: Developing a new approach. *International Coaching Psychology Review, 8*: 89–91.

Whatley, M. (2011). A new model for family owned business succession. *Organization Development Journal, 29*: 21–32.

Index

For Product Safety Concerns and Information please contact our EU
representative GPSR@taylorandfrancis.com
Taylor & Francis Verlag GmbH, Kaufingerstraße 24, 80331 München, Germany

www.ingramcontent.com/pod-product-compliance
Lightning Source LLC
Chambersburg PA
CBHW050654280326
41932CB00015B/2904